So What

Felicia Young

Copyright @ 2021
By Felicia Young

So What

All Rights Reserved- No portion of this book may be reproduced, copied, stored or transmitted by any person or entity in any form or by any means, graphic, electronic or mechanical, including photocopying, recording, scanning or by any information storage or retrieval system, without prior permission in writing from the publisher.

ISBN: 978-1-7365339-0-1

Printed in the USA by Felicia Young

Request for publication should be submitted to
FeliciaYoungInc3@gmail.com

**Cover design by
Chelsea Markray
"Chelsea Miss Artist"**

DEDICATIONS

This book is dedicated to:

My Children
Nadria, Dalya & Jermal Jr. – MY personal **So What** motivation
who are the reasons I keep going

My Inner Circle & So What Team:
Dr. John R. Adolph, Charity Martin, Opal Morris, Shatonna Rucker, Mary Simon, Sherrie Charles, Schemika Rodriguez, Jackie Sanders, Arlicia Albert, Betty Graham, Alfred Beverly II, Kim Hardy, Antoinette Hardy & My Mom –
who helped me stay focused on the reason why
I needed to tell the story

My So What Readers:
All the people who are assigned to my journey in life

So What

CONTENTS

Sydney

7

Olivia Rose

21

Waverly

32

Harmony

46

Ashlyn

58

Tiny

71

Stuck in the Past

How many times have you had dreams of an extraordinary, wonderful, and magical life? Dreams to start your own Fortune 500 Company? Dreams of returning to college to earn your degree? Dreams to marry your knight in shining armor and raise an army of loveable kids? Dreams to travel the world to make an impact in the lives of millions? Dreams of creating limitless opportunities for a more meaningful life?

But to your dismay, your dreams have yet to come true simply because you spend too much time living your life through the obscured lenses of your past. Mistakes you made in your teenage years paralyze you from accomplishing your goals today. Betrayal and hurt cause you to live your life hidden behind an impenetrable structure more immovable than the Great Wall of China, leery of letting anyone near you again. Allowing the opinions of others to determine your worth and value. Torture and abuse by the hands of someone who said they loved you that left you shattered and broken. The narrative of your past is prohibiting you from living the life you were destined to have.

Yes, you have been bruised. Yes, you have been devastated. Yes, you have been mistreated. Yes, you have been heartbroken. Yes, you suffered a significant loss. Yes, you are distraught. No one alive has escaped being hurt emotionally at some point. But you cannot let what happened in your past stop you from moving headfirst towards your future. You cannot let the fear of starting over cripple you and overpower your desire for a fresh start. You cannot let the pain of your former life have a stronghold on you and prohibit you from exploring your passions. It is time for you to stand up to hardships from your past. It is time for you to face your fears head-on. It is time for you to be the overcomer that you are. It is time for you to move forward and live the life that you longed for.

You are about to meet six extraordinary women whose journeys will inspire you to move full steam ahead. These six remarkable women have stories that may resemble yours. They lived unimaginable hells, but with courage, determination, and an irreplaceable support system, they overcame the odds that were stacked against them.

Meet **S**ydney, **O**livia Rose, **W**averly, **H**armony, **A**shlyn, and **T**iny.

Six remarkable women who, despite the hardships in their lives, looked their pasts in the face, shouted "**SO WHAT**".

So What

Sydney

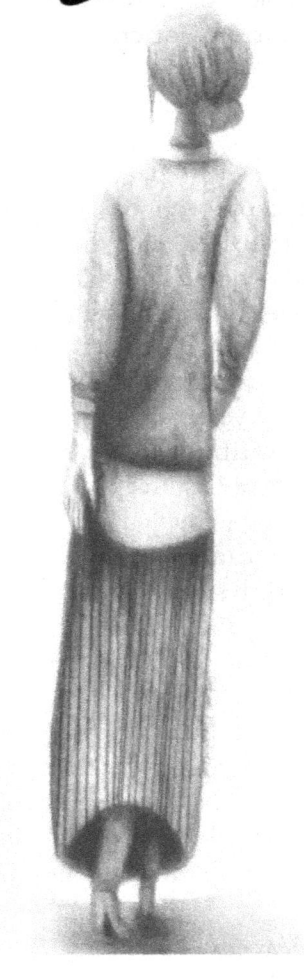

So What

Sydney

"You look beautiful, Mommy!" Sydney's fifteen-year-old daughter, Monica, exclaimed.

"Thank you, love." Sydney bent down and kissed Monica on the forehead, then returned to putting on her makeup. Sydney stared at herself in the mirror. She had to admit she was nervous. Tonight, was the first night in ten years that she would see her classmates. West Port's class of 2006 produced some very successful individuals. Lawyers, actresses, financial planners, athletes, and judges. Everyone in her class seemed to have accomplished the goals that they had set. Everyone but her. Although she graduated with her class, Sydney did not continue her education. She did not feel that she could. By the time Sydney graduated from high school, she already had three children. College was not an option for her. She had to work to provide for her children. During high school, she missed out on so much. While her friends enjoyed school dances and football games, she was busy changing diapers and working to feed her babies. While her friends were going away to college and pledging fraternities and sororities, she was nursing high fevers and attending school plays. Sydney felt as if she was stuck in a dead-end life. She watched her friends excel while she struggled to make ends meet. Sydney complained to her friends all the time about how bad her life was. They tried to encourage and offer options to her, but she never seemed to think she could be more than what she was. Sydney was a young single mom with three kids, two jobs, and no degree. As her ten-year reunion rapidly approached, she had no desire to attend. She dreaded being around her successful classmates and having them look at her disapprovingly at being who she was. After months of pleading, her friends finally were able to convince her to attend. As she stared at herself in the

So What

mirror, she critiqued every part of her body. She always criticized herself. She never felt pretty. Or smart. Or desirable. Or loved.

Her doorbell rang. Lori, Bethany, and Lizette barged inside her home and gave her a big hug. They were her best friends from childhood who were there for all three of her children's births. They were there to wipe every tear away after her children's fathers left her. They were there to babysit when she had to work overtime. They were there in the hospital holding her hands while she recovered from a suicide attempt. They had been a vital part of her life for as long as she could remember. It had been over a year since she had seen all of them together. She was beyond thrilled to spend time with women who she considered sisters. The friends piled into Lizette's SUV and made their way to the hotel where the class reunion was held. After they parked, the ladies walked arm in arm into the ballroom, where they were greeted by flashing lights, loud music, and friendly hugs. Sydney was pulled to the dance floor by Charles Freeman, the school's mascot. Sydney and Charles were great friends. Charles tutored Sydney and helped her graduate from high school. He was determined to make sure she did not fall behind in her studies. He saw an extraordinary woman who just needed an ally in her corner to keep her on track. When Sydney did not believe in herself, Charles did.

The old friends spent hours laughing and dancing. They talked about the wonderful things that were going on in their lives. Lizette made partner in her law firm. Bethany was recently engaged and moving into an exclusive neighborhood with her fiancé who was a councilman. Lori's seventh book just made the best sellers list. Charles was an accomplished administrator at their local university. When it was Sydney's turn to brag on her life, she complained about every aspect. From her dead-end jobs to her deadbeat children's fathers. According to Sydney, nothing ever went right in her life. The more she complained, the more her friends began to roll their eyes and get fed up. In between sips of his drink, Charles sternly stopped her, "Honey, you complain way too much for my nerves. You have way too much to be grateful for. You need to thank God every day for keeping your family healthy and cared for. If you don't like how your life is going, maybe you need to do a reality check and make some changes. Now PLEASE stop all that complaining. You're killing my buzz." Sydney was stunned by her friend's harsh tone, but Charles was right. She spent so many years complaining about all the wrongs in her life that she never thought about what she needed to do to make improvements.

So What

Several days later, Sydney arranged to have lunch with Bethany. They met at Mack's Diner, a place they used to hang out at when they were younger. They would spend hours there talking and sharing their dreams. Sydney could not get Charles' comments out of her head. She wanted a better life for herself and her children. But she had no clue where to start and how to overcome her fear of trying. Bethany stared intently into her friend's eyes. "You need to face your demons. You have issues that are stopping you from seeing yourself the way those who love you see you. Maybe you need to speak to a therapist to help you sort through your past and help you make plans for your future. When I get depressed or lose my way, I spend time with my therapist. She's helped me tremendously. I strongly suggest that you see her".

Sydney was extremely nervous about meeting Dr. Kinroy. She had not talked to anyone besides her best friends about her past. However, she was tired of feeling like she was worthless. Sydney wanted to be a role model for her kids. She wanted a career. She wanted a husband. She wanted to be happy. But could she ever have that kind of life? A single woman with three kids and no degree. Can a person like her really become successful? When Sydney met Dr. Kinroy, she was in awe. Dr. Kinroy was a stunningly tall and beautiful woman who had a warm smile and a compassionate disposition. Dr. Kinroy started with small talk. Asking Sydney about her children, her current life, and what she hoped to gain from their sessions together.

"My name is Sydney. I'm twenty-eight years old. I've never been married. I have three children, ages fifteen, thirteen, and eleven. I work two jobs and I'm tired. I know there is more for my life, but I don't know what it is and how to get there. I don't know if I even deserve to have a good life. I've made so many mistakes, so many wrong turns, and I don't know if I will ever be more than what I am now." Dr. Kinroy stared at Sydney.

"You were thirteen when you had your first child? Were you raped?" Dr. Kinroy asked with intense concern.

"No, ma'am. I was not. He was fourteen."

"You have been through quite a lot in your life I see. Having sex at such a young age is not normal. I need you to tell me your story. Start from the beginning and leave nothing out".

Sydney took a deep breath and began her recount of a life filled with pain and tragedy. When Sydney was growing up, she was a daddy's girl. She loved her father

So What

more than she loved anyone else in the world. He was a hardworking man who provided for her mom and step sister. Even though her sister was for another man, Sydney's dad treated her as his own. They lived in a lovely subdivision surrounded by other homes with manicured lawns. Neighbors walked their dogs. Children rode their bikes up and down the street. Sydney's dad made sure his family felt safe and secure in their surroundings. Sydney's dad was a great protector and so much fun to be around. He made sure he took time to teach his girls about life. He constantly praised them and told them that they were the most beautiful girls in the world besides their mother. He reminded them daily that they could be anything they wanted to be and could have anything they wanted to have if they worked hard for it. Sydney's dad was her hero.

When Sydney was nine years old, her world was shattered. She was working on an art project with her classmates in an after-school program when her teacher approached her and led her to the principal's office. Her aunt was waiting for her. Her aunt scooped her up and hugged her tight. "Baby girl, I have to bring you to your mommy." Sydney's aunt could not stop crying as she drove to the hospital. She held Sydney's hand tightly as she led her to a hospital room. Sydney heard screaming inside the room. She slowly walked in to see her uncles, grandmother, and sister crying uncontrollably. Her mom was laid across the hospital bed, hugging someone. As Sydney walked closer to the bed, her heart pounded. She did not understand what she was seeing. Why was her daddy lying in bed? Why were his eyes closed? Why was there blood all over his clothes? What was going on? Sydney's mom looked up at her. "He's gone, baby. He's dead".

Sydney's dad wanted to surprise his wife with a new diamond bracelet. He took Sydney's sister with him to help pick out the perfect piece. Sydney's sister giggled with excitement as their dad told her how he would surprise their mom during dinner that night. Sydney's sister asked if they could walk down the street to get ice cream before they went home. Against his better judgement, he let her sister get a double scoop of strawberry ice cream. He said if he gets in trouble for ruining her appetite for dinner, he was going to blame her. Sydney's sister laughed uncontrollably as she licked the melting ice cream. Sydney's dad held her sister's hand while they walked to their car. Sydney's sister's ice cream flew out of her hand when someone knocked her to the ground. As she struggled to stand up, she saw a look of fear on her dad's face. The man who knocked her down held a gun to her dad's head and demanded the bag that held her mom's new bracelet and her

So What

dad's wallet. Her dad gave the thief everything that he had in hopes that they wouldn't be hurt. The thief gave Sydney's sister a sinister smile as he caressed her face. Sydney's dad became enraged and lunged at the thief. Both men fell to the ground. Sydney's dad punched the thief twice before a loud noise stopped him in his tracks. Sydney's dad's body became limp and he fell face down on the ground. His blood slowly flowed from his chest towards the melting ice cream next to him. Sydney's sister let out a blood-curdling scream and the thief ran away. Life, as their family knew, was changed forever.

Days leading up to the funeral, scores of people visited their family to bring food, offer condolences, and keep the family company. Sydney's mom had to be sedated. She could not wrap her mind around the fact that she would never see the love of her life again. Sydney did the best she could to console her mom, but the pain of her hero being murdered was heart-wrenching. How would Sydney survive without him? Who would protect her family? Who would make her feel like the princess that he always said she was? Who would love her? On the day of her dad's funeral, Sydney could barely breathe. She laid in bed while her family got dressed. Her aunt peeked in her room to check on her. She sat next to Sydney and began to stroke her hair.

"You'll be alright, baby. Your dad was a rare man who loved you all to pieces. You have to remember all of your good times with him. Remember everything that he taught you. You have to be strong, Sid. He wants you to be strong. Now here. Take one of your mom's pills. It'll help your nerves. We're here for you, Sid. Your family is here".

Sydney swallowed the pill and laid down a few more minutes before she got dressed. As she walked to the funeral car, she felt the pill kick in. She began to feel numb. Her aunt helped her into the car and they drove to the church. Sydney felt a person on each side of her. They helped her walk towards her dad's casket. As she got closer, her heart began to pound. He looked like he was sleeping. He was so handsome. There was no way he was dead.

"Daddy?"

"Daddy?" Sydney began to tap on his body to wake him up. "DADDY!!!!!" Sydney became hysterical. Her uncle had to carry her out of the church and eventually took her home. Sydney fell asleep and did not wake up until the following day. Sydney was allowed to miss a few days of school. She laid in the bed with her mom and sister staring blankly at the television. Her mom took pill

So What

after pill to keep herself numb. Her mom never wanted to feel anything again. Although her mom was there physically, mentally, she was gone. Sydney began to sneak her mom's pills. She did not want to feel the pain of her grief, either. At the young age of nine years old, Sydney became addicted to pain pills. She missed her dad dearly. Sydney missed how he made her feel special, beautiful and like she could conquer the world. She longed for that feeling again. As she got older, she began to look for this feeling in the boys in her school. Derek was a year older than her. He was fine. He did not love her, but he did like the way she let him feel her. Several months later, she gave birth to Monica. Her teachers and counselor reported Sydney's mom to child protective services claiming neglect for Sydney's pregnancy and suspected drug addiction. Sydney's aunt stepped in to help raise Sydney and her sister while their mom received therapy to help her live through her pain.

Even though her family had begun to come to terms with her father's death, Sydney had not been able to cope. She became promiscuous and more addicted to drugs. Sydney was desperate to find someone to love her as much as her dad. When she could not, she smoked, snorted, or injected anything that would help the pain go away. Nothing helped. Sydney's best friends, Lori, Lizette, and Bethany, tried their best to help her get through her grief. They encouraged her to participate in positive activities. They tried to keep her busy so she would not dwell on her issues.

Eventually, Sydney seemed to find a light at the end of the tunnel. She began to enjoy time with her friends. She began to flourish in her academic life. She began to feel normal again. When she became pregnant with her second child, her friends were shocked. Sydney never revealed who the father was and started to feel her life spiraling down again. Sydney's friends were determined to help her overcome her agony. They helped her keep up with her assignments. They took turns babysitting her children while she completed her homework. They never once doubted that she could keep moving forward despite the mistakes she was making. The school mascot, Charles, was from a wealthy and prominent family. Charles was determined to help his friend as much as he could. He talked to his family about Sydney and asked what could be done to help her. His father set up a meeting with Sydney's mom and aunt. He expressed his condolences to them and said that he would like to pay for Sydney to attend counseling sessions to help her deal with her grief. Charles would tutor her so she would not get behind in her

So What

classes. Sydney began to see a future for herself. She no longer felt hopeless. Being surrounded by her best friends and close family pulled Sydney out of the depression she had been trapped in for years.

Sydney was allowed to work a part-time job in a family friend's store. She was happy to help her mom with bills and take care of her children. Charles still tutored her to make sure she stayed on the honor roll. He had always been focused on school and his future. He always stayed on the A honor roll. He knew which university he wanted to attend. He knew he wanted to be an educator. He knew he was destined for greatness while helping others. He always encouraged his friends to do their best academically. He firmly believed in having a strong circle to pull the greatness out of each other. He believed in Sydney. He started talking to Sydney about college and life after graduation. He felt that she should be a counselor. She had been through so much in her life that her story would allow her to be compassionate and helpful to others who experienced grief and life struggles. This possibility excited Sydney. She fantasized about going to her office wearing name brand suits and shoes - looking through her files in a fancy briefcase.

"Your dad would be very proud of you, Sid," her mom told her one evening as they sat on the sofa together watching a game show. "He always wanted you to go to college and be more than he and I ever were. You are making us both proud."

"Are you sure I can do it? Even with two kids?" Sydney asked.

"Why not? You're very smart. You're focused. You're surrounded by family who will help you raise OUR kids. You're going to college, lil lady, and there's nothing left to say about it". Sydney laughed and kissed her mom's cheek.

Sydney's sixteenth birthday was rapidly approaching. Her mom enlisted the help of Sydney's best friends and Sydney's aunt to make this a surprise party to remember. Sydney thought she was going to grab pizza with some classmates. Charles picked her up and presented her with a dozen white roses. Sydney burst into tears. Her dad always presented her with white roses on special occasions. Sydney gave Charles a long hug and kiss on his cheek. Charles was an invaluable friend. They climbed into his truck and drove to the secret location. Sydney gave a big smile as she realized what was happening. She saw her friends lined up outside, yelling surprise as she stepped out of the truck. She hugged everyone and posed for pictures. Sydney's friends led her inside. In all of her life, she has never seen a room so beautiful. There were white roses strategically placed around the room. Photos of her dad and her were on easels at the entryway. A strobe light

So What

blinked with her favorite colors. Tables of food lined the wall. A DJ had music blaring with the latest hits. Everything was perfect. Sydney realized she had not seen her mom or aunt yet. Charles said they needed to pick up her gift and would arrive soon. Sydney and her friends danced the night away. This was the best night of Sydney's life.

Lizette grabbed Sydney and pulled her off the dance floor. She had tears in her eyes as she led Sydney outside. Lizette said that she received a phone call from Sydney's mom's phone, but it was not Sydney's mom. It was a police officer. He dialed the last number called. He told Lizette that there was a horrible accident involving the owner of the phone and another female passenger. A drunk driver ran a red light and plowed into Sydney's new birthday gift. There were no survivors.

By the time Sydney turned seventeen, she had her third child by a third man. She sporadically went to school and barely held on to jobs. Sydney suffered from severe depression and did not see a way out of her living hell. Her parents were gone. She did not feel she had anyone to guide her or love her. She began to neglect her kids and stopped caring about life altogether. Sydney isolated herself from her friends and began to spiral out of control. Although the home that Sydney was raised in was left to her sister and her in her parent's wills, Sydney could not bear to live there. She and her kids were homeless, taking turns living in homeless shelters, horrible cheap hotel rooms, or vacant houses. The memories of her dad and mom haunted her. The pain she felt was unbearable. She decided that she could no longer go on living. Sydney reached out to Charles. He dropped everything he was doing to meet Sydney at the park. His eyes watered when he saw his once beautiful friend transformed into someone unrecognizable. She had lost so much weight. Her clothes did not fit. Her hair was matted. Her eyes were dark and sunken. The light from her soul was gone. Charles squeezed Sydney tight. He kissed her gently on her forehead. He sobbed for her. Sydney admitted that she was struggling and having a difficult time caring for her children. She asked if Charles and his family would mind caring for her kids for a few days until she could develop a game plan. She wanted to spend time in her family home with her sister and get the house ready so she and her kids could move in. Charles eagerly agreed.

Sydney stood in front of her childhood home. Tears streamed down her face as memories flooded her mind. Vivid memories of her dad teaching the

So What

neighborhood kids how to play kickball in their front yard and the yells from her mom every time that red rubber ball trampled her rose bushes. Vivid memories of her sister and dad cutting the grass with the riding lawn mower as she and her mom grilled steaks in the backyard. Vivid memories of her dad butchering her ponytails when she needed to take school pictures and her mom was away on a business trip. Vivid memories of intense family love. She adored her parents. She missed her parents. She knew that she could never provide that type of love for her kids. She knew that she could never make those kinds of beautiful memories with her kids. She was too broken to give them the love they deserved. Charles' family could. Sydney found an old family portrait. She was four. Her sister was seven. Her parents looked in love. She walked into her parent's bedroom. Sydney wrapped herself in the blanket on their bed. She then opened the bottles of sleeping pills that she brought with her. She took one pill at a time until the bottles were empty. She laid her face on the family portrait and closed her eyes for what she hoped to be the last time.

Charles tried calling Sydney to see how she was doing and to see if she needed help getting the house ready for the kids. She would not answer. He had a strange feeling that something was wrong. Charles called the police and had them meet at her home. Sydney's car was in the yard, but the doors to the house were locked. Charles rang the doorbell and banged on the door. The police walked around the house and peered through the windows. To their horror, they saw Sydney sprawled out on the bed, surrounded by empty bottles of alcohol and pills. The paramedics rushed Sydney to the hospital to be treated for her drug overdose. She was placed on a suicide watch. Her best friends took turns staying with her and watching her children. Sydney was in for a long recovery. One evening, Charles walked into her room. He stood by the door for what seemed to be an eternity. He watched his friend stare off in space with dry tear marks on her face.

"So many people love you, Sid. Especially your kids. Why can't you see that?"

Sydney did not move. Fresh tears flowed. Charles walked over to her and planted a long, loving kiss on her forehead. "Sid, what would your dad think seeing you living like this? Even though he wasn't in your life long, he planted enough seeds inside of you to grow better plants than this. I know I can be brutal and blunt, but clearly that's what you need right now. You got to snap out of this and do better. If not for yourself, for those kids. Do you want all three of them to live a life feeling like you do because their mother chose to take her life and leave them

So What

helpless? If you don't want to do it for your kids, do it for the memory of your parents. Sid, your dad was the best man I've ever met. He was my hero too. Yes, I have an amazing family, but it was something about your dad that set me on the path I'm on today. He planted seeds in me too. He told me I could make a difference in the world. That I can be an influential man. A strong man. A man's man. He made me see that I am here to do great works in the world and I take that assignment seriously. I was lost when he was murdered, but I hear his words in my ears all the time. I live by those words. I get angry at you because I know you were able to spend more time with him and received more words of wisdom than I did, but you're choosing to ignore what he told you. He wanted you to be more than what he and your mom became. He wanted you to experience the best that life had to offer. He worked his butt off to make sure you and your family were taken care of while he was alive and after his death. He would not be happy with you right now, Sydney, and you know it. If he knew how you mistreated HIS grandbabies, girl, you know you would have hell to pay. I love you. You have so many who love you. We're here for you and we want to see you smile. So get it together and let's do this".

Charles was determined to see her graduate with them. He brought her schoolwork to her and helped her improve her grades. With the push of Charles and her best friends, she remained focused. To her surprise, her school counselor told her that she was graduating from high school. Walking across the stage was an accomplishment that Sydney never thought would happen. She did it. Her children were cheering her on. Her daughter, Monica, handed her a bouquet of white roses and kissed her on the hand. "You did it, mommy. Mommy gradu…gradua…. Mommy did it!" Sydney laughed and kissed her daughter's forehead and said, "We did it, baby. Yes, we did". Sydney smelled the roses and hoped her dad and mom were smiling down at her.

While her friends went off to college, Sydney continued to work two jobs. She had dreams of more. Working to help others wearing tailored- made suits. But they would just have to remain that… dreams.

As Sydney finished relaying her story to Dr. Kinroy, she wiped tears from her eyes. Dr. Kinroy smiled at her gently and spoke.

"Sydney, you experienced such a traumatic childhood. The fact that you are here to tell your story is remarkable. You are remarkable. For you to keep moving forward despite the cards you were dealt shows that deep down inside, you are a

So What

survivor and destined for greatness. You need to stop letting your past hurts cripple you. Yes, you faced tragic deaths. Yes, you had three children by three different men. Yes, you were addicted to drugs. Yes, you were addicted to alcohol. But **so what**!!! You are still here. You have three amazing children who think of their mom as their hero. You are still young and important. You matter! You did not go through all the hell you went through not to tell your story. You have amazing friends who have always pushed you towards your destiny. They have always believed in you. It is time for you to start believing in yourself. What do you want to do for a career?"

"Ironically, I would love to be a counselor."

Dr. Kinroy laughed and said, "Well lil lady, let's get a game plan together for you to become Dr. Sydney."

After her session, Sydney called Charles. He let out a happy scream as his best friend asked for his help to enroll her in college and help her earn her degrees.

"You look amazing, Mommy," Monica said as she watched her mom put on her cap and gown. Sydney was graduating from college with honors and she could not hold back her tears as she walked into her living room filled with her children, friends, and sister. As the announcer called her name, she walked across the stage with a big smile on her face. She knew her mom and dad were proud. They said she could be anything she wanted to be and they were right. She had officially become Dr. Sydney and she was ready to help others overcome the devastations in their lives. On her first day at work, she walked into her office and took a good look at herself in her full-length mirror. She was wearing a jet-black designer suit and shoes, holding a black briefcase. As she walked to her desk, she was surprised to see two dozen white roses staring back at her. One bouquet was from her best friends who wished her well with making a difference in the world. The other bouquet was from her children, with a card that said they thank God every night for blessing them with a strong mom who fought all odds to make a better life for them.

Then YOU said........... **So What**

Do you see any part of yourself in Sydney? Explain:

What obstacles did you face when you were young that cause you to feel stuck now?

So What

Who is your support system? What roles do they play in your life?

What steps do you need to take to have the life you deserve? Are you willing to focus on those steps?

What are you willing to say **So What** to regarding your career?

So What

Olivia

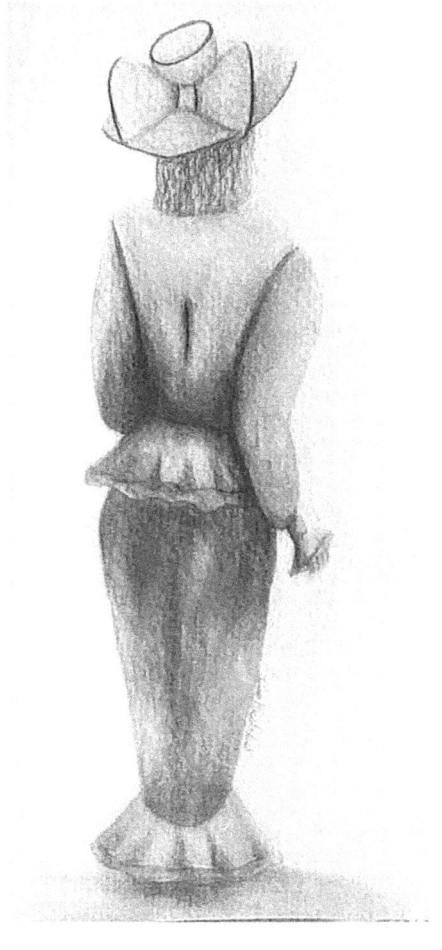

So What

Olivia Rose

"SURPRISE!"

Olive Rose and Daniel smiled from ear to ear. Their family and friends pulled off the ultimate party, a surprise fiftieth wedding anniversary celebration. Olivia Rose was on top of the world. As she and Daniel walked hand in hand around the ballroom, greeting everyone, Olivia Rose could not help staring at him. For fifty years, she was married to the love of her life. Olivia Rose met Daniel when she was seventeen years old. After dating four short months, they got married and started a family. Daniel was old fashioned. He believed men should work and take care of their family and women should stay at home and take care of the household. Although Olivia Rose had dreams and ambitions to be a career woman, she did not argue with her husband. Olivia Rose and Daniel had five beautiful children who grew up to have wonderful families of their own. Olivia Rose raised her children and her grandchildren, who all turned out to be successful in their own way. Olivia Rose was proud of her family and her husband.

Olivia Rose and Daniel held each other tight as they danced. Olivia Rose whispered in his ear how much she loved him. He kissed her on her cheek and held her closer. Olivia Rose knew she was a lucky woman to be able to spend the rest of her life with the love of her life.

"I'm not in love with you anymore."

Those words knocked the wind out of Olivia Rose. She did not comprehend what Daniel was saying. The night before, they celebrated their wonderful life together. Now over breakfast, he shattered her world.

"Livey, I'm sorry. I have to be honest. I have not been happy for many years. I stayed out of obligation to you and our family, but I'm being unfair to myself. I'm leaving the house to you and the car. I'll be back this evening to pack my things.

So What

Don't hate me, Livey. Trust me. This is for the best. Eventually, you'll find someone to love you."

Daniel slid an envelope to Olivia Rose and walked out of the house. Olivia Rose opened the envelope. Tears streamed down her face as she realized she was holding divorce papers. Three hours later, Olivia Rose was sitting in the same spot in front of a cold plate of breakfast and those papers. She had not heard her phone ring repeatedly nor the doorbell.

"Mother, mother. Mother what's going on? I've been calling you for hours". Olivia Rose's daughter, Amber, was standing at the kitchen door trying to get her mother's attention. Olivia Rose picked up the envelope and handed it to Amber.

"What the hell?" Amber sat across from her mother in total disbelief. She immediately called her three brothers and sister to come to their parent's house. Amber helped her mother into the bathroom to get cleaned up. Then she gently led her mother to the backyard. Olivia Rose always found happiness in her backyard. That is where she spent many years watching her family play and enjoy themselves. As each of her children arrived and Amber gave them an update on what their awful father did, Olivia Rose's children showered her with hugs, kisses, and lots of love.

"How could that bastard do this to you?" Daniel Jr. asked.

"Watch your mouth, DJ!" Olivia Rose barked.

"Excuse my language, Mama. But I don't understand it. He could've done this month's ago before we spent all that money on that fake party last night."

Everyone stared at Daniel Jr. in disbelief.

"Really, DJ. THAT'S what you're angry about?" Amber hissed at him. Daniel Jr. shrugged his shoulders and shook his head.

"What reason did he give you for leaving?" Olivia Rose's youngest daughter, Nicole, asked in between tears.

"He said he hasn't been in love with me in years. He said I gained too much weight. I stayed around the house too much. He was always stressed behind our bills, and I never contributed anything to the household. He said he wasn't attracted to me anymore. He said since all of the kids and grandkids were grown and taken care of, he didn't feel obligated to take care of me any longer."

Daniel Jr. yelled, "That's bulls…. Sorry, Mother. That's insane. HE'S the one who demanded you be a stay-at-home wife. HE forced you to quit college mid-semester when you decided to go back after we all were in school. HE forced you

So What

to quit your part-time job so you could be home for us after school and have his meals cooked. HE'S the one who gained weight. Mother! YOU are gorgeous. You look like you're in your thirties instead of sixty-seven. I will NOT allow him to tear you down. You will get through this bulls….. sorry Mother. You will get through this with us behind you."

Olivia Rose gave her kids a huge smile. Although, her husband's words cut her to the core, she believed what her kids said. She was an amazing mother and wife and she took excellent care of her family. Olivia Rose's youngest son, Landon, sat in silence. Amber noticed how quiet he was and asked if he was alright. He shook his head and said no. He glanced at his mother and told her something that she never would have suspected in a million years. Landon told his mother that the love of her life had been having an affair for over seven years. The mistress was Daniel's lawyer. Landon caught them together years ago. Landon confronted his dad and demanded he end the affair immediately. His dad gave him an evil laugh and told him not to tell Olivia Rose or it would kill her. Landon kept that horrible secret for years so as to not devastate his mother.

Olivia Rose blew a kiss to Landon and apologized for him being put in that terrible position. Nicole told her mom that she would help her get a game plan together to ensure she received everything she deserved and more in the divorce settlement. Daniel Jr. gave a sinister smile and told his mom that he and his law firm would happily represent her.

"We're going to take that basta… sorry, Mother. Take him to the cleaners."

Over the next few days, all of Olivia Rose's children helped her sort through mounds of documents. She had no clue they still owed so much on their mortgage. She had no clue that the monthly notes were so high. She had no clue they were behind on bills. She had no clue they filed for bankruptcy. She started feeling stupid. When he told her to sign documents, she never read them. She just always trusted her husband's business sense. Daniel Jr. learned that his dad's mistress had been helping him hide assets for years so he would not have to pay Olivia Rose anything when he decided to leave her. Daniel Sr. underestimated his son's brilliant legal mind. Daniel Jr. filed motion after motion and document after document to seize assets from his father. This process would definitely take time.

In the meantime, Olivia Rose needed to find a way to generate income. She worked on a resume and applied for all the jobs that paid the amount of money

So What

she needed to pay her bills. Unfortunately, her phone never rang for a final job offer.

"I don't understand. I applied for over twenty jobs and I haven't heard back from any of them." She sat in her rocking chair in the backyard, talking to Amber. Amber was too focused on going through mounds of bills and writing checks to pay for them out of her own account.

"Amber. Amber. Stop writing checks and help your mother figure this mystery out".

"Sorry, Mother. You know I have a one track-mind. Ok let's see. Let me see your resume." After Amber read through the one-page summary of her mother's work experience, she glanced up.

"Don't get upset when I tell you the truth. You're applying for jobs that require more skills and education than you have. You're competing with kids who are fresh out of college with master's degrees who grew up learning the latest technologies. You're going to have to apply for jobs that don't mind that you have no college degree or your only experience was being a homemaker. Then figure out what career you want and enroll in some courses to get educated in that field. You have five kids who adore you and we will pitch in to help with your bills until you can get settled. And don't you dare tell me no. You've sacrificed your whole life for us, including our father and this is the least we can do to help."

Olivia Rose began to apply for any job that had vacancies. She got a job as a waitress in an upscale country club. She really enjoyed her job. She was a people person with a dynamic personality. She catered to her customers and made sure they were well taken care of. That special attention she gave them turned into high tips. With the help of her children, Olivia Rose was able to develop a realistic budget and pay down the mountain of debt that her soon to be ex-husband left her with.

Olivia Rose looked forward to the upcoming weekend. Her children and grandchildren made plans for a bar-b-que at her home. They all had not been together in quite a while and she was excited to hear laughter in her home instead of the deafening silence that she had gotten used to. On the day of the bar-b-que, Olivia Rose's manager asked if she could stay a couple of hours over. They were short-staffed and a large law firm called to reserve space for a late luncheon. Olivia Rose agreed. She could use the extra money and she would still be home in time for her family. Olivia Rose was so focused on setting the table and making sure

So What

the arriving customers were seated and comfortable that she nearly missed who had sat at the table with the law firm.

Apparently, it was an appreciation luncheon and the selected lawyers were allowed to bring their spouses. To Olivia Rose's horror, there was an elegant looking lawyer who had her arms wrapped around Daniel. Daniel looked at Olivia Rose and gave her a weak smile. Daniel's lawyer/mistress realized who Olivia Rose was and gave Daniel a long kiss on the lips and wrapped her arms around him tighter. Olivia Rose wanted to run out of the restaurant in tears, but her pride refused to let them see her upset. Olivia Rose went overboard with treating the entire table kindly. She made sure they were well taken care of, including Daniel and his lawyer/mistress. Every time Olivia Rose approached the table, the lawyer/mistress went out of her way to be affectionate to Daniel. At first, Olivia Rose was bothered by the sight but she soon realized that the lawyer/mistress was intimidated by Olivia Rose. Both ladies noticed how Daniel stared at his wife every time she brought a plate to the table or refilled a glass. The way she treated the table was how she treated her family for years, with kindness and genuine care. He missed the way she cared for him. When the luncheon was over, one of the partners thanked Olivia Rose for her excellent service and hospitality. He rewarded her with a $350 tip in addition to what they already gave on the bill. Olivia Rose thanked him and continued to clear the table.

"It was good seeing you, Livey. You look beautiful." Daniel said as his lawyer/mistress grabbed his arm to lead him out the door.

"Have a good evening, sir." Olivia Rose replied as cold and disconnected as she possibly could.

Her children could not help but laugh hysterically as Olivia Rose retold the story at dinner. They agreed that Daniel was full of regrets and the lawyer/mistress would not have peace in her relationship with him.

"She will always be unsettled as long as she's with him. She knows that if she was able to get him to cheat on his wife of fifty years, then it's nothing to stop him from cheating on her". Landon said in between bites of chicken. "We're very proud of you. You're handling this divorce better than we thought you would. How do you feel?"

"I have my moments when I don't want to get out of bed. I cry a lot. I think I'm mourning or going through those stages of grief. I get angry a lot because I dedicated my life to my family. I dedicated my life to my husband. And for him to

So What

try to make me feel like my devotion was a hindrance to him is unacceptable. I have times when I throw myself a huge pity party, but then one of you kids would call or stop by and jolt life back into me. You are the loves of my life. Now, I want some more of that delicious chicken. And pass me some peach cobbler."

Several days later, Olivia Rose was assigned to a table that was filled with senior citizens wearing matching orange shirts. In casual conversation, she asked who they were. They were an organization who called themselves the Seasoned Citizens Coalition. They were comprised of people age fifty-five and up who used their experiences with life to help others get on their feet. The group consisted of widows, veterans, illness survivors, former addicts, and divorce survivors. They offered counseling services, job readiness programs, job placement programs, and recreational activities.

The program director invited Olivia Rose to attend their next mixer to explore her options for her life after divorce. Olivia Rose was nervous and unsure when she arrived at the community center. But that uncertainty quickly turned into excitement when she entered. The group greeted her with warm hugs and smiles.

The program director led her into the multipurpose room filled with lively people around her age. During an ice breaker game, each person had to tell their story of overcoming obstacles. Olivia Rose was impressed by the triumphs of her new friends. When it was her turn to speak, she did not quite know what to share seeing as how she felt she had not overcome anything.

"I was married for fifty years. I have five wonderful kids and eight amazing grandkids. I was a stay-at-home mom. I never finished college or worked. I'm not familiar with how to operate computers. I'm far from being tech-savvy. To be honest, I have no marketable skills and feel I lack the experience to have a real career."

"You're being hard on yourself, lady." A suave looking man named Morgan walked up to her. "You wouldn't have survived this long without some type of skills. You said you were a stay-at-home mom. What are your kids' professions?"

"Amber is a registered nurse. Daniel Jr. is a partner in his law firm. Nicole is a lawyer in Daniel Jr.'s law firm. Mitchell is an orthopedic surgeon. Landon is my youngest child, and he's currently working on his Ph.D."

The room stared at her in amazement.

Morgan gave a loud laugh and said, "Looks like you have plenty of experience at something. You raised some pretty accomplished kids."

So What

"Yeah, but that's not getting me any jobs that I've applied for. I don't have a college degree. I don't have any work experience outside of my home. I'm not as sharp as the kids coming out of college. There is too much competition and I don't qualify for high paying jobs. I'm sixty-seven years old with no marketable skills."

Morgan stared at Olivia Rose in disbelief. "Have you been that brainwashed? **So what** if you have no college degree. **So what** if you don't know how to work computers. **So what** that you're an older person starting your life over. If you have the determination to be better, you will find a way to make it happen. That's what our organization is about. Giving people like you the resources they need to be who they want to be. You raised five successful kids. That means you obviously have incredible management skills. I remember how you treated us at the restaurant. You have excellent hospitality skills. You also seem to have great people skills. There is no reason why you can't have a career based on your experience alone. We'll help you find your niche and find a career that deserves you." Olivia Rose smiled and for the first time in a long time, she felt valued.

On the day of the final divorce hearing, Olivia Rose stared at herself in the mirror. Today would mark the end of an era. She expected to cry hysterically and be an inconsolable mess, but surprisingly, she was calm and at peace.

Daniel Jr. strolled around the courtroom with confidence as he addressed the judge.

"Your honor, my client, Mrs. Olivia Rose, spent all of her adult life caring for her family. The written agreement between Mrs. Olivia Rose and her husband allowed her to be a stay-at-home mother who took care of her husband and children while her husband provided for the family financially. It was her husband who swore to support their family until death do them part. Mrs. Olivia Rose held up her end of the deal and we're requesting that the court requires him to do the same."

Daniel Sr.'s lawyer/mistress objected and asked for any type of proof to show that there was an agreement for Daniel to provide for Olivia Rose until death. Daniel Jr. smiled and presented a greeting card that Daniel Sr. gave Olivia Rose on their thirtieth wedding anniversary. Inside the card, he wrote:

"My dearest Livey. I am amazed that God has blessed me to have a soul mate like you. You have made every day of my life more incredible than the day before. You are a fantastic mother and an excellent wife. Life without you is unimaginable; therefore, I promise I will do everything in my power to keep you happy and in

So What

love with me. I will always be your protector and provider as long as we both shall live. That's the least I can do to repay you for making me the happiest man in the world. I love you today and forever. Your husband, Daniel."

Daniel Sr. held his head down and fought back tears as he struggled to forgive himself for cheating on his wife. Olivia Rose let tears fall freely down her cheeks. The tears were a release that was long overdue. She was not sad. She was not angry. She was not bitter. She was overwhelmed with happiness as the judge granted the divorce and awarded Olivia Rose a lump sum of money from the stash that Daniel Sr. tried to hide. It was enough to pay off her home and all the debt that Daniel left her with. There was plenty of money to allow her to continue to stay at home, but Olivia Rose wanted more for her life. She became a recruiter and empowerment speaker for the Seasoned Citizens Coalition. She was responsible for turning the lives around of seniors who were forced to restart their journeys but had no idea where to begin.

"Hi. My name is Megan. I'm sixty-one years old. I was an alcoholic for forty-eight years. I didn't finish high school. I never held a real job. Never kept a meaningful relationship. I've been sobered for a few years, and I want more for my life. But I don't think I can have a better life because I'm just too old."

Olivia Rose smiled, gave Megan an intense stare and said, **"So what!"**

Then YOU said………. **So What**

Do you see any part of your life in Olivia Rose? Explain:

Have you allowed yourself to heal and move forward from a devastating breakup?
If no, what will it take for your breakthrough?

If yes, how did you overcome your hurt?

Do you share your past experiences as a way to help others?
Describe 3 times:

What are you willing to say **So What** to regarding starting over?

So What

Waverly

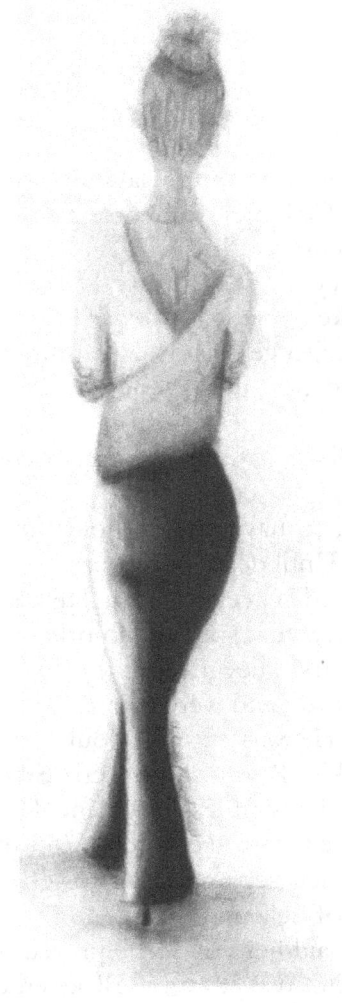

So What

Waverley

"I, Blake, take you, Waverley, to be my lawfully wedded wife. To have and to hold, from this day forward, for better, for worse, for richer, for poorer, in sickness and in health, until death do us part."

Waverley stared into the eyes of her husband to be. Tears slowly trickled down her face. She wanted to make a mad dash towards the door and escape from this hell. As flashes from the audience's cameras captured what appeared to be the perfect picture of a bride and groom, Waverley took a deep breath and swallowed hard.

"I, Waverley, take you, Blake, to be my lawfully wedded husband……"

Deep breath.

"From this day forward, to have and to hold, for richer and for poorer. In sickness and in health……. Until death do us part."

Blake's vicious stare pierced Waverley's soul. He knew that she did not want to marry him, but Waverley knew that she had no other choice. Waverley and Blake dated off and on for eight years. They met at the wedding of a mutual friend. Both were a part of the wedding party and were paired to walk down the aisle together. Blake was very handsome. He was six foot four. Two hundred and thirty-two pounds. Perfectly smooth skin. Pearly white teeth. Smooth shaven head. A body that should grace the cover of any fitness magazine. He was very wealthy and well connected. He appeared to be the perfect catch. After their friend's wedding, both of them should have gone their separate ways for good but instead, they started dating and her personal life of hell began.

As Waverley unwillingly said her vows, she prayed that her married life would be better than her engaged life. Waverley and Blake entered the reception hall and smiled from ear to ear as their family and friends cheered them on. Blake twirled

So What

Waverley until they reached the center of the floor for their first dance. He kissed her gently on her heart-shaped lips and held her tight. Blake loved his wife with all of his heart. He knew they would be together until death took one of them.

"You're my everything. I know you know that. I will take care of you forever. Just make sure you take care of me. Don't ever make me look like a fool or I'll ki…… I love you, Waverley. Just remember that."

The lump in Waverley's throat stayed planted uncomfortably. She managed to whisper a weak, "I love you more." Waverley made her way around the room, hugging and kissing her guests. She loved her family and friends so much. She spotted the most important person in her world and quickly ran over. Waverley's mother, Suzette, was her hero. After Waverley's father died, her mother became the provider for their family. Even though she worked two jobs to make ends meet, her mother made sure she stayed active in Waverley's and her sisters' busy lives. Her mother created an atmosphere of peace and love within their home. She instilled virtuous qualities inside each of her daughters. She taught them how to be ladies who had high standards for their lives. She taught them the essential values they would need to have successful careers. She taught them how to be desirable women for their future husbands. Waverley adored her mother and had always done anything to help her, even if it meant marrying the evilest man ever created.

"Your dad would be so proud of you, honey. You are such a beautiful bride. I want to dance. Wheel me to that floor."

Waverley pushed her wheelchair-bound mother to the dance floor and they both giggled as they moved to the beat of the music. Tears formed in Waverley's eyes as she enjoyed the look of happiness on her mother's face. Blake walked over and kissed Suzette on the cheek and asked if he could interrupt their dance. He took the handles of Suzette's wheelchair and used it as a dance partner. Suzette threw her head back with laughter as her new son -in-law danced with her. Waverley sat at the table with her sisters. She was the oldest of the four and a second mother to them. When their mother worked, it was Waverley who made sure their meals were cooked and homework was done correctly. She made sure she took care of her family. That is what her dad would have wanted. Her sisters graduated from high school and college. They had productive careers and started their own families with incredible men. Waverley was the last to marry.

So What

"You don't look happy, sissy. Who do I need to beat down?" Waverley's baby sister, Nicole Ann, knew Waverley way too well. Nicole Ann was the feisty sister who took no crap from anyone.

"I'm good. Just ready to get out of this dress." Waverley lied the best she could. Nicole Ann rolled her eyes and headed to the food table to get a slice of cake.

"Congratulations, beautiful."

Waverley jumped out of her seat and into the arms of her first boyfriend, R.J. She had not seen him since she graduated college. When they were kids, Waverley and her sisters spent summers at R.J.'s family farm in the country. They had so many great memories. R.J. held Waverley tight around her waist and kissed her on the cheek. Waverley felt an intense pain under her arm. She turned to find Blake gripping her and pulling her away from R.J. Rage filled his eyes.

"Um, babe. This is my childhood friend, R.J. We used to spend summers in the country with his family. He's the one I told you who went to the military and has been living overseas." Blake let go of his grip and gave R.J. a handshake and tense smile.

"Can I speak to you outside, my lovely wife?"

Blake led Waverley to the terrace. As soon as Blake closed the door and Waverley turned around, she felt a painful sting across her face. Blake slapped her so hard that she nearly fell to the ground.

"Don't you ever disrespect me like that again. You better make sure I know every man that you know. And they don't need to grope on you at all!"

"He's my friend."

SMACK!

"Did I tell you to say anything? Go to the restroom and get your face together. Then get back to this reception so we can finish celebrating."

Blake reentered the reception and Waverley stood stunned outside. After she regained her composure, she joined her guests and pretended to enjoy herself. As she had done so many times before, she faked her way through the night.

Waverley could not wait to meet her mother and sisters for their monthly Sunday brunch. She had not seen them since she arrived back from her Caribbean honeymoon. As she walked into the restaurant, she could smell the enticing aroma of Italian sauces and bread. Waverley loved this restaurant. When her dad was alive, he used to treat the family to dinner here once a month. She was glad they kept this tradition. Her sisters squealed when they saw her. They ran towards her

So What

and gave big hugs. Waverley winced in pain. Hopefully, her sisters did not notice. Waverley smiled when she saw her beautiful mother at the table. Waverley bent over and planted a big kiss on her forehead.

"What the hell are those?" Nicole Ann asked angrily. When Waverley hugged her mother, her shirt rose to expose fresh bruises on Waverley's back.

"Girl, the other night I was drunk and tripped down some stairs. You know I can be clumsy."

Nicole Ann lifted Waverley's shirt and fussed, "those look like fist prints, not stair prints! Waverley, is Blake beating you? Do you need us to kill him?" Nicole Ann was so serious about the last question that it made Waverley bust out laughing.

"Girl, no. I'm fine. Couples get into arguments. That's part of marriage. I appreciate the concern but seriously, I'm fine."

Waverley's mother put her head down for a moment. She had something she needed to say, but this was not the right time. Waverley told her family of her amazing time in the Caribbean. She and Blake swam in the ocean. They went horseback riding. They danced the night away in different clubs. They made love under a blanket of stars on the beach. Waverley painted a heavenly picture of their honeymoon. She purposely left out the hell that accompanied them. Just as often as Blake swept Waverley off of her feet, he would also make sure he kept her beaten and tortured. He became enraged when Waverley smiled and thanked the concierge for carrying her bags. His blood boiled when Waverley left an extra tip for the helpful college student who was their waiter during brunch. His skin crawled as men did a double-take whenever Waverley walked by. No matter how much Waverley tried to reassure Blake that she only had eyes and never-ending love for him, he still found excuses to cause her physical pain.

After brunch, Waverley wheeled her mother to Nicole Ann's car. She bent down and kissed her on her cheek. Her mother hugged her tightly and whispered, "I love you very much. You have to get away from him immediately. I'll help you."

Waverley stood up and glanced nervously from her mother to her sisters. Nicole Ann helped her mother get secured in her car. She folded up the wheelchair and carried it to her trunk. She motioned for Waverly to help her. Nicole Ann placed both of her hands on Waverley's rosy cheeks and kissed her nose. Then sternly said, "We love you, sissy. You are everything to us. To see you in pain is ripping us apart inside. Make some time to talk to me. I need to know what's going on and I will help you any way I can."

So What

Salty tears stung Waverley's eyes. She had no clue that her family knew about the abuse. She tried so hard to cover it up. She could not leave Blake. That just was not an option for her. She owed him so much and he would make sure she never forgot it.

Blake came home angry from work, and nothing that Waverley tried could settle him down. He went to the kitchen and grabbed a cold beer out of the refrigerator. He walked into his media room, where he got comfortable in his recliner and began to watch his favorite football team play on television. Waverley walked slowly into the kitchen and began to prepare a meal for them both. She grilled sirloin steak, sautéed onions and mushrooms, steamed broccoli florets, and baked sweet potatoes. She baked homemade lemon cupcakes with lemon icing. The aroma from the kitchen filled their home. Everything on Blake's plate was placed perfectly with care. She walked into the media room and placed his meal in front of him on a tray. She walked back into the kitchen to grab her food and another beer for him. As she walked inside the media room, he started yelling at her. He preferred his steaks cooked medium-well. She accidentally cooked it well done. He took his plate and threw it at her. Hot food burned her face and shoulders. He leaped out of his chair and grabbed the food tray. He slammed the tray against her back until she collapsed on the floor. He sat on her chest and pinned her arms down with his knees. He grabbed the steak and tried to shove it down her throat. Waverley tried her best to free herself. She gasped for air as she began choking on the sizzling meat. Waverley turned her head to the right and threw up on Blake's imported carpet. Blake started yelling at her for ruining his room and began slapping her repeatedly. Blood from her bust lip slowly trickled down her face. As if a switch was flipped, Blake stopped the beating, climbed off Waverley's chest, and gently lifted her up. He wrapped his arm around her waist and slowly kissed her neck.

"Why do you hate me so much?" She asked as she wept.

"I don't hate you. I'm in love with you. You are the most stunning woman in the world and you're mine. All mine …. Until death."

Time passed by and her marriage got worse. No matter what she did, Waverley could not stop Blake from abusing her.

"I'm pregnant." Waverley was excited as she told Blake. He always wanted children. A house full. Surely this would turn their marriage around. Blake grabbed his wife and gave her a tight warm hug. He took her by her face and gave her the

So What

most loving, sensuous kiss. In all the years that she has known him, that was the first time he has ever been so passionate with her. Yes, their marriage was about to get better.

Waverley's family enjoyed shopping with her to fill the baby's nursery with the many items needed and quite a bit of things that were not needed. Blake came home daily with a smile on his face. He made sure Waverley was well taken care of. Blake made her relax often. He cooked her meals. He showered her with attention. They spent hours laughing and talking about their future. Waverley was ecstatic. She became head over heels in love with her husband and she was glad that her life was finally perfect.

Waverley woke early one Sunday morning to the sound of the doorbell. It was too early for anyone to visit. She looked through the peephole to see who was on the other side. A middle-aged woman was standing outside the door. Waverley cautiously opened the door only to find two small children holding tightly to this woman's legs.

"May I help you?"

"I need to see Blake."

"May I tell him who you are?"

"Tell him his children's mother."

Waverley held tightly to the door. She tried her best not to faint. Waverley closed the door and stormed to Blake's media room. Blake looked confused as he tried to understand what she was yelling about. A few minutes later, Waverley heard Blake and that woman talking sharply at one another. Then the front door slammed. Blake walked back into the media room, holding both children by the hand. Waverley blinked her eyes rapidly in confusion.

"These are my children. They'll be staying with us for a few weeks."

There was no number of beatings that Blake could ever give to cause the amount of pain Waverley felt at that moment. She stared at the children who were the spitting image of their father, her husband. She slowly walked out of the room and into her bedroom. She laid in her bed and sobbed uncontrollably. She felt stupid. Dumb. Worthless. Enraged. Lifeless. She was fed up. After Blake made his children breakfast and got them comfortable watching television, he went to try to explain to Waverley. He got angry that she would not accept his apology. He took her arm and yanked her out the bed. He started to shake her as he yelled his apology. Waverley squinted her eyes and stared at him with intensity. Rage boiled

So What

within her and all the hatred that she felt for him rose inside of her. Waverley kneed him in between his legs so he could let go of his grip on her. She grabbed the lamp off of the nightstand and bashed him with it. She knew she could not beat him up, but he would definitely know he was in a fight.

This Sunday was Sunday brunch day. Waverley's family patiently waited for her to arrive. Nicole Ann called her nine times and the phone went to voicemail each time. The family sensed something was wrong and rushed to Waverley's home. Her car was in the driveway and so were several police cars. Nicole Ann rang the doorbell repeatedly. Waverley's neighbor opened the door. Nicole Ann looked anxiously at the grisly scene that stared back at her. Blood was splattered on the floor and wall. Two small children were lying on the sofa crying. Police were preoccupied with processing the scene.

"What the hell is going on? Where is my sister and who are those kids?" Nicole Ann screamed.

The neighbor looked sadly at Nicole Ann and told her Waverley was rushed to the hospital and the kids were Blake's.

Nicole Ann sped to the hospital. She hurriedly pushed her mother's wheelchair down the hallway as her sisters ran in front of her. They thought maybe their sister went into labor early and did not have time to contact them. When they arrived in her room, they were met with a horrific sight. Waverley laid in the hospital bed connected to tubes and beeping machines. Her eyes were purple and swollen shut. The right side of her face was the size of a baseball. She was missing teeth. Her left arm was in a cast. Her stomach was flat.

A police officer was standing over Waverley writing notes in a notepad. After the officer finished taking Waverly's statement, her family circled her bed as she recounted what happened. Blake admitted to having an affair. His children's mother was tired of being a single parent and wanted a break. The children's mother often called Blake to ask him to help share custody, but he would not agree. He did not want his wife to find out about his secret life, so he paid his children's mother more money to hire a nanny and he went to spend time with his children without Waverley knowing. This was unacceptable to his children's mother and she decided to shake up his perfect world by unexpectedly showing up at his home and leaving the kids. Waverley tried her best to fight off Blake after she hit him with the lamp. Her strength was no match for him. He grabbed her by her shirt and flung her across their bed. As she stammered to stand up, he stormed

So What

towards her and hit her with his fist. She crashed into the wall. She kicked him again and he fell to his knees in pain. She ran out of the bedroom and to the hallway closet. She grabbed the wooden box from the top shelf and opened it. Blake grabbed her by her hair and tossed her to the floor. She heard his youngest child screaming. She heard his oldest child asking for help on the phone. She heard three loud blasts. There were screams, confusion and chaos as Waverley became unconscious. When Waverley woke up in the hospital, the doctor delivered a series of bad news. She had a concussion, broken bones, and a lacerated liver. The beating she received from Blake caused her to miscarry. Blake was currently in surgery to remove bullets from his body. Waverley shot him three times and doctors were unsure if he would survive.

Waverley's mother sobbed uncontrollably along with her sisters. Nicole Ann kissed Waverley's bruised face and asked why she stayed in that abusive relationship. Waverley took several slow deep breaths and began to tell a story that sent the room into shock.

As Waverley and her sisters grew up and started to develop their own lives, Waverley's mother no longer had to work two jobs. The women enjoyed their monthly brunches, vacations, and time together. Seemingly out of the blue, Waverley's mother developed a life-threatening degenerative disease that left her permanently ill and wheelchair-bound. Waverley contacted the best doctors around who were unable to provide a cure but were able to provide medication to ease her pain and symptoms as well as provide her with home health care nurses to assist with her needs. The cost of this new lifestyle was exorbitant. Waverley promised her mother that she would take care of the costs and not to worry about anything. Little did her family know, Waverley began to swim in debt. She downsized her home and vehicle to cut expenses. Waverley began to work multiple jobs to keep up with her mother's mounting medical bills. She did not want to ask for help from her sisters because they had bills of their own and she was the one who promised to take care of their mother. After she met Blake, she told him why she worked so many jobs and so many long hours. He was infatuated with and falling in love with her. He offered to take some of the financial burdens off her if she would become his girlfriend. Waverley thought he was joking until she received a receipt in the mail one day saying her mother's home health care services were paid upfront for the next year. The pressure that took off Waverley's shoulders was undeniable and she was eternally grateful to Blake. The two began dating and

So What

fell in love. She found out that he was possessive and had jealousy issues, but she was unbothered because she was in love with only him and had eyes for no one else.

The first time she tasted blood in her mouth was after they got home from a concert. Blake overheard a stranger call her sexy as she walked by. Even though Waverley never heard the stranger, Blake felt that she should not dress provocatively. She rolled her eyes and said she was a grown woman who would dress any way she felt. He grabbed her by the arm, swung her around, and slapped her face. She landed on the floor, dazed. She jumped up and lunged at him. He grabbed her by the throat and slammed her against the wall. He whispered slowly in her ear. "If you EVER talk like that to me again, I will kill you. If you EVER disobey me again, I will stop paying for your mother's treatments and she will die!" From that day on, Waverley remained obedient and beaten in order to save her mother's life.

Waverley's mother started fussing at her in between tears. She could not believe Waverley stayed in an abusive relationship behind medical bills. Nicole Ann fussed at Waverley for thinking she needed to care for her mother by herself. With as many children as Suzette had, each of the girls would have pitched in to cover the expenses. Nicole Ann told Waverley that as soon as she got out of that hospital bed, she needed to file for divorce, move in with her, and develop a game plan to take care of their mother. For the first time in a long time, Waverley felt relief in her life. Although her physical and mental bruises would take time to heal, she felt optimistic that she would recover one day.

A soft knock was heard on the door. The doctor walked slowly to Waverley and said he had some news. Blake's injuries were too severe and he died on the operating table. Nicole Ann looked at the doctor and in an icy cold tone, said, "**So what?**"

After Waverley was discharged from the hospital, she moved into Nicole Ann's home. She felt mentally drained from the thoughts of losing her baby. Her mother and sisters worked overtime to love on her and walk through the healing process with her. She was determined to get stronger each day. One beautiful afternoon, she made herself comfortable in Nicole Ann's living room next to her mother. They laughed together as they watched their favorite movie on television. The doorbell rang and a delivery man handed Nicole Ann a certified letter for Waverley. Blake's attorney was attempting to reach her to finalize the wishes of

So What

Blake's will. Waverley's mouth dropped in total disbelief. Blake had a trust fund set up for each of his children. He made special provisions for Waverley's mother's medical care for the rest of her life. He left the remaining of his multimillion-dollar estate to Waverly.

Four years later, Waverly walked down the aisle again. This time, she smiled from ear to ear. This time, her heart tingled as she made her way to the love of her life, her childhood boyfriend. This time felt right. As the flash of camera lights captured her pure joy, Waverly grabbed her husband to be's hand and proudly said:

"I, Waverly, take you, R.J. to be my lawfully wedded husband…"

Then YOU said……….. **So What**

Do you see yourself in Waverly? Describe:

If you have ever been in an abusive relationship, why did you stay?

Are you able to move on to new relationships without bringing your past traumas with you?

Do you recognize and listen to warning signs to steer clear of dangerous relationships?

So What

What are some non-negotiables that you desire in a healthy loving relationship? Name 5

What are you willing to say **So What** to regarding new love?

All relationships have ups and downs. That is just a part of life. However, physical and mental abuse is NEVER acceptable. Love yourself enough to know you do NOT deserve to be mistreated. If you find yourself in an abusive relationship, SEEK HELP.

So What

Harmony

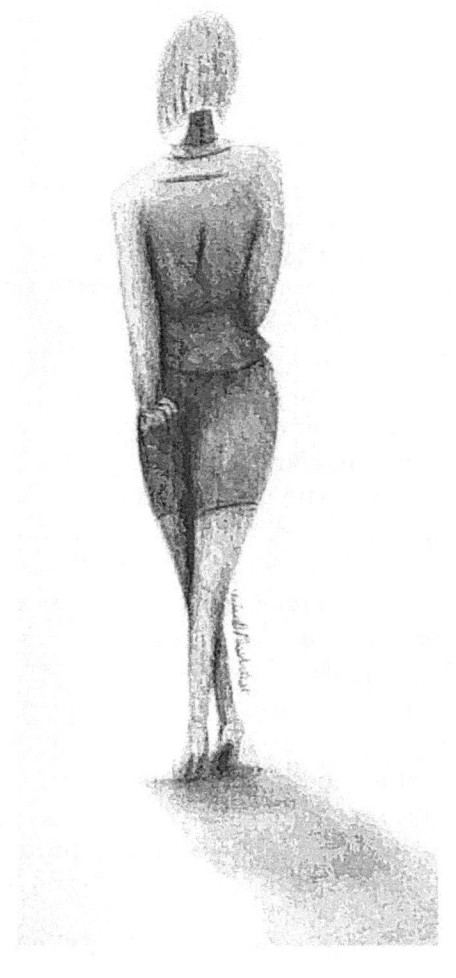

So What

Harmony

Harmony Anderson was an intriguing woman. A stunning, smart, ambitious, and mysterious woman who had a past that could threaten to destroy her career at any given moment. Harmony lived in a small town. She developed a reputation as someone who would do anything to get what she wanted. She did not care who she walked over or hurt along the way. Harmony was determined to be on top of the world by any means necessary. Harmony had no problems burning bridges. She was not a woman to look back. Harmony graduated from high school and was accepted to her local university with a full scholarship under a cloud of suspicion. It was an unspoken fact that Harmony used her seductive talents to achieve whatever goal she set for herself. Harmony loved her life. She loved the attention she received. She loved the men who catered to her and gave her all of her heart's desires. Harmony's world was amazing. That was until the night she turned on the news and saw her face plastered on her big-screen television in connection with a murder-suicide. She was forced to relocate and change her life forever.

Ever since she was hired as the chief executive at the prestigious Johnson & Associates marketing firm, she developed thick elephant-like skin. In this male-dominated corporation, she knew that she had to portray that particular no-nonsense wholesome girl persona. She had to be taken seriously. Out of the seven applicants who interviewed for that position, most were cutthroat men who had worked for J & A ever since they graduated from Ivy League schools. They had expectations of rising up in the ranks and being promoted to top positions throughout the firm. They spent years doing some serious butt kissing trying to impress the partners to solidify their place in this multimillion-dollar conglomerate.

With the untimely death of Michael Johnson, the chief executive for the past seventeen years, the wolves quickly mourned then prepared to take his place any

way that they could. Being assigned to this position would mean going from a medium five-figure salary to a high six-figure salary with commissions and bonuses, a luxury company car, access to exclusive restaurants, clubs, and trips. A lifestyle that was envied by the wolves.

On the day of the interview, the wolves came ready to impress and undermine their competitors. While waiting their turn to interview in the conference room, they half-jokingly criticized each other. They brought up each other's past mistakes on major projects while exaggerating the success of their own mediocre projects. Their pissing match was briefly interrupted when they saw Harmony walk off the elevator. Their eyes were mesmerized by the way her hips swayed left and right in a fitted pencil skirt. Her long sleek legs pranced with confidence with the help of those electric blue four-inch stilettos. She wore an electric blue satin blouse that subtly showed her 42-double d's. The wolves watched as Harmony spoke to the receptionist, who politely pointed to the conference room. The wolves were so busy fantasizing about Harmony that they did not realize that she walked into the conference room and was immediately called into the partners' office for her interview.... for THEIR job.

Two months after being hired as the head woman in charge, Harmony still felt the wolves' vicious backlash. They challenged her every decision in meetings. They went behind her back to secure deals in hopes that the partners would take notice and replace Harmony with them. They even had the audacity to suggest to anyone who would listen that the only reason Harmony got the job was that she was great on her back and used her skills to seal the deal for employment. Although she could have easily slept her way up the ladder to become a partner, she chose not to. Harmony prayed that her past reputation would not catch up with her and ruin her life. She loved her career but hated the way her colleagues, male and female treated her. This industry was small and the competition was stiff and she knew she would have to maintain a certain image if she wanted to climb the ranks.

Harmony was excellent at her job. She was the firm's superstar, landing major contracts with large-scale companies across the country. Although Harmony gained the respect of her superiors and was requested specifically by clients, she was well aware that she was despised by many of her colleagues who were envious of her success. They just did not understand how she came out of nowhere to become the face of one of the top marketing firms in the country.

So What

Harmony was successful, wealthy, and powerful. Even with all of this, she was lonely. She had to be selective about the company she kept. She could not trust anyone out of fear of hidden agendas from people looking to see her fail and fall.

There was one person who caught her attention. He was one of the men being interviewed for the position, but he was not a wolf. His name was Shawn Garrett. Shawn was very nice to Harmony. He came to her defense when others ripped her to shreds. He made efforts to befriend her and make her feel comfortable. Harmony appreciated him and became sexually attracted to him. But her guards had to stay up and her legs down. She thought he had to have ulterior motives for wanting to be around her. Everyone else did.

On a late fall evening, the entire sales staff was summoned into the board room by the partners. There was an unusual excitement in the atmosphere as the rumor of the possibility of landing the most significant contract in J & A history spread throughout the office. This contract was with a multibillion-dollar international company called Tate Technology owned by the renowned brilliant twins, Jason and Mason Tate. Each sales associate was being given a chance to pitch a marketing campaign that would launch the Tate family's latest technology venture. Harmony was thrilled and frightened at this opportunity. On one hand, she knew she would create the best campaign the firm has ever seen. On the other hand, she knew the wolves would do anything in their power to make sure that did not happen.

She had to remain focused. She only had two weeks to deliver the most important masterpiece of her career. She came to work early. She stayed late. She poured her heart into her work. While she was busy typing on her computer, a familiar ding alerted her to a new email. It was from Shawn: *Don't spend so much time trying to make a living that you forget to live. Lunch?*

Well, that was a pleasant surprise. What the hell, why not?

Harmony met Shawn downstairs and they took a stroll a few blocks to Gio's, a friendly family-owned eatery. They were seated in a booth and ordered. She had Ziti pasta, a garden salad, and an ice-cold glass of peach Bellini. He ordered seafood Alfredo, garlic bread, and a bottle of Italian soda. While they waited on their food to be delivered, Shawn was making small talk. Harmony could not focus on his conversation because she was entranced by the way his lips moved. The way his hazel-green eyes squinted when he smiled. This man was fine, she thought. She had to remain professional and composed, but the woman within her was very

So What

intrigued by him. How long had it been since she was with a man? Too long, that's for sure.

Back in her college days, she never went more than two days without going on a date. She always had a rolodex of men who she could call at the drop of a hat. Harmony was a well-known freak. Single or married, young or old, male or female, it did not matter to her. She had an appetite unlike no other and her goal in life was to satisfy her urges any time with anyone with a price of valuable gifts and money.

Her favorite "anyone" was Reginald Johnson, a wealthy business owner who did not mind splurging on Harmony. He spent thousands of dollars to wine and dine this sex-obsessed beauty. Although Reginald was married with children, it did not stop him from seeing her and getting careless with their romance. Reginald's wife found out about his affair and exposed Harmony as the home-wrecking whore that she was. Pictures from a private investigator showed Harmony and Reginald together, leaving lavish hotels wrapped in each other's arms, sitting cozy by each other at expensive restaurants, and kissing one another in jewelry stores. Copies of every salacious picture were sent to Harmony's parents, her job, her church, plastered in the grocery stores, and on cars in her neighborhood. Harmony was horrified and humiliated. But nothing could compare to the pain and dismay that she felt when she turned on the evening news to hear about a sadistic murder-suicide of a prominent local family.

Reginald's wife had enough of him cheating on her with Harmony. She confronted him after receiving a call from the hotel stating that she left her three-carat diamond ring on the nightstand and it would be kept safely until she was able to get it. Reginald's wife calmly walked into Reginald's study and asked if he was in the hotel. Reginald stuttered and denied doing anything wrong. Reginald's wife walked out of the room then returned with the envelope containing the stunning ring. Reginald stared at her, then apologized. His wife slowly lifted the gun he bought her for her birthday. Reginald begged and pleaded with his wife to spare his life. He swore his love for her. He tried to reason with her. Reginald's wife could not get the pictures of her husband's lips on another woman's body out of her mind. She did the only thing that would stop him from ever cheating on her again…she shot him in his heart. As reality sunk in about what she had done, she became grief-stricken and angry. She placed the gun to her head and pulled the trigger. A suicide note was found and Harmony Anderson was named as the reason

So What

for the tragedy. That was a horrible time in her life that she had yet to recover from.

Harmony was brought back to reality when the waiter brought their food. Shawn was still talking and she was glad that he did not notice she had spaced out. She had not thought about Reginald in a long time. But it did force her to stop her promiscuous, gold-digging ways.

She had fun at lunch with Shawn. He was great company. Funny, charming, smart, and sexy. Harmony watched his perfectly shaped lips blow to cool his pasta. She wondered if he was a great kisser. She had to force herself to focus. After their lunch, they lazily walked back to work. Harmony sat at her desk. She could not stop thinking about those lips.

Harmony ended up working until after 9 pm. She heard the cleaning crew yell to her that they were leaving. She took a break from her computer. She leaned back in her leather chair. She closed her eyes and started fantasizing about those perfect set of lips. She wanted to know more about him and decided to stalk his social media page. She gazed at pictures of him in a tuxedo at a political event, in basketball shorts on the court, kayaking, skiing, and horseback riding. He was a very active man, a very sexy and apparently a single man. Harmony noticed there were no pictures of a wife or girlfriend. Nor any other family members. She began to wonder out loud, "He must have a hundred girlfriends, and that's why he doesn't have any pictures up. It figures. He's too sexy to be with just one woman."

"It's not good to judge a book by its cover, ma'am."

To her surprise and horror, Shawn was standing at her door, enjoying the entire show.

He stared at her briefly. He casually walked over to her chair. He bent down and lifted her chin, and gently pressed his lips against her. Harmony began to feel tingly. She positioned herself to explore Shawn more, but as quickly as he entered her office, he was gone just as fast.

Harmony went home with many questions and fantasies. She convinced herself to let her guard down with him just once.

The next day, she arrived at work with a little extra pep in her step. She could not wait to see him. She had to play it cool, of course, but she was making out with him on the conference table in the middle of their staff meeting in her mind.

By lunchtime, she had not seen him and she could not stop thinking about him. She went against her rules and sent him a nonchalant email: *Dinner?*

So What

Two hours later and no reply. Harmony fussed at herself for letting her guard down. How could she be so stupid? Really Harmony???

She forced herself to focus on her campaign. She had only four days left to finish. If she won the contract for the firm, she would be promoted to partner and her salary would triple. What a great opportunity.

At 4:43 pm, she heard the familiar *DING*.

It was Shawn. Dinner at 8. He would pick her up from her home. For the first time in a long time, Harmony got off at 5 pm. She went home to get ready. Harmony poured a glass of wine, turned on some music and twirled to her closet to find the perfect outfit. She turned on the Jacuzzi tub and took off her work clothes. She stared at herself in the mirror while sipping on her wine. She was excited about tonight.

As she soaked in her tub and sipped from her glass, she could not help but think of all the possibilities of being in a relationship with him. From dressing up to attend fancy events to him teaching her to play the sports he loved, Harmony felt that she could definitely be in a relationship with him. The doorbell jolted her. She glanced at the clock. O wow! It was 7:36 pm. She wrapped herself in a towel, took a sip of wine and rushed to the front door. It was Shawn. He looked so sexy. He wore a black crew neck sweater and dark denim jeans. Subtle smelling cologne. And that smile.

She apologized profusely for not being ready and asked if he could give her twenty minutes to get dressed. She walked into her bedroom. She headed for her closet to grab her short red spaghetti strap dress and black shawl. She took off her towel and slipped on her dress. She turned around to look at herself in the mirror and was startled to see Shawn leaning against her door, watching her. She walked slowly towards him, wrapped her arms around his neck, then attacked those perfectly shaped lips. She glanced at the clock: 12:23 am. So much for dinner. He got dressed and walked to the door. They kissed for a few minutes and he left.

The next morning, Harmony walked into her office to find a bouquet of flowers sitting on her desk. The note said, "thanks for changing my life." Now she knew she was great in bed, but life-changing sex? That was a new compliment to her.

She only had three days left to finish her presentation, but she was nearly finished. She turned on her computer and clicked to open her file. Nothing. No file. Anywhere. She began to panic. Her computer was wiped clean. She did not know what happened.

So What

She remembered she backed up some of her presentation on a memory stick that was at her home. She rushed to get it and would spend the next two nights finalizing it.

She noticed that she had not seen or talked to Shawn since that night. That did not matter now. She needed to nail this presentation and nothing could distract her.

She had an 11:30am appointment with the partners and the Tate brothers. She was very confident when she walked into the conference room. She looked amazing and she nailed her presentation. She thanked the panel for their time and ended with a beautiful smile. The Tate brothers looked at each other uncomfortably and asked what was going on. The partners were angry and dismissed her. Harmony was confused. She went to her office and waited to hear from any of the partners. A few hours later, she was summoned to the conference room. She walked in and saw the partners, the company attorney, and Shawn. What was he doing there? He had a subtle smile on his face.

Harmony sat down with a look of bewilderment on her face. Mr. Simon expressed his disappointment in Harmony. He said he has never seen the prospect of more money and a promotion cause someone with as much talent as her to resort to theft and plagiarism. Harmony was stunned. Theft? Plagiarism? What were they talking about? She looked at Shawn. He gave her an icy cold stare. What was going on?

She let her guard down, that's what. Flashbacks whisked through her mind as Mr. Simon was chastising her. Shawn was so nice to her. He was helpful. He took up for her. He was her friend. He made love to her. He used her! He was not a wolf. He was a manipulative lying shark. Shawn knew he had no chance of being promoted within the company, but he had ambition, a strong desire to be a partner, and the ultimate ulterior motive: to destroy her.

When he saw Harmony in the interview room, he immediately recognized her as the person who ruined his life. He also acknowledged that she was brilliant. He knew that if he were able to get close to her, he would be able to use her to get himself promoted and destroy her life. Never once did he dream it would be this easy.

The night he caught her in her office looking through his pictures, he was actually sneaking into her office to steal her presentation. While watching her, he got the idea to seduce her enough to let down her guards. It worked easier and

So What

faster than he thought. Harmony was drunk when Shawn went to pick her up for dinner. She thought she was sipping on a glass of wine when she actually gulped down a bottle... on an empty stomach. Not only did she unwisely have sex with Shawn, she was quite loosed lipped when it came to details of her presentation and the password to her computer. The flowers with the thank you note were a semi sarcastic appreciation for access to the presentation of a lifetime. The presentation that would triple his salary, make him partner in the most prestigious marketing firm and destroy her career.

She realized she had not seen him for a few days. His going missing was his eagerness to present "his idea" to the Tate brothers. After he left her home that night, Shawn went back to her office and stole her work. He deleted every file on her computer. He met the Tate's at their corporate office and wowed them so much that they agreed that he would be their campaign representative. They only came to listen to the other presentations out of respect and courtesy of the staff's hard work, especially the superstar they heard so much about. To their horror and dismay, Harmony "stole" Shawn's hard work. She tried to convince them that it was her original idea and Shawn stole it from her. They asked if she had documentation or proof to support her claim. She had none. The partners fired Harmony and told her to clear out her office and vacate the building immediately. Harmony was devastated and stunned.

How could he? Why did he? Why did she let her guard down and raise her legs up?

She quickly boxed up her personal items and was escorted by security out of the building. She opened her trunk to put the box in and when she closed the door, she was startled by Shawn. He had an intense look of hatred on his face. She reached out to slap him. He grabbed her arm and smiled.

"What did I do to you to make you ruin my life?" she asked. He walked close to her and whispered, "You killed my parents."

"Your parents?"

"Reginald and Melanie Johnson."

Harmony got weak. "But your last name is Garrett!"

"My middle name is Garrett. I changed it to my last name after you murdered my parents so I could have a chance at a normal life." Shawn spent years trying to forget the tragedy of his parents' death. When Harmony walked into the interview that day, he instantly recognized her face from the hundreds of pictures that his

So What

mom spread throughout their city. Shawn knew she did not know who he was. He took time to devise a scheme to destroy her. But ruining her career was not enough. His rage started building and he grabbed Harmony by her throat. He did not just want her fired. He wanted her dead. His loving mother suffered while this slut stole his father away. Shawn's life was devastated by his parents' death and she was the reason. She had to pay. Harmony could not pry his hand from around her throat. She felt herself getting weaker and almost blacked out. Security guards saw the attack on camera and rushed to save Harmony. Shawn was immediately arrested.

Harmony sat in the security office with tears rolling down her face. The guard on duty asked her why the attack happened. Harmony retold her past and blamed her promiscuous lifestyle for destroying three lives. Harmony did not see how she could ever recover. Her reputation was ruined. There would be no way another company would hire her with all the negative press that was about to expose her. The life that she always dreamed of was destroyed. The guard let out a laugh in disbelief and nonchalantly said, "You're telling me that just because you slept around a lot all those years ago, that you won't be able to get a job today? I'm not trying to be ugly, but what's between your thighs is not that powerful, sweetie. You were young and you made mistakes. I'm sure you learned your lesson. You can't let the negative choices from your past stop you from making a beautiful life for yourself. And if no one will hire you based on what happened years ago, **so what!** Start your own company and blow them out the water!"

Five months after Harmony was fired from her job, she received a knock at her door. Her former supervisor, Mr. Simon, stood at her steps with a plant and a look of sadness. He apologized for ever doubting her integrity and begged her to come back to work for the firm. She thanked him for his time and generosity, but she turned the job offer down. She decided to start her own marketing firm and be her own boss. She told Mr. Simon that it was good to see him, but she needed to excuse herself to meet with her clients … the Tate brothers. Mr. Simon's jaw dropped as she escorted him out the door.

Harmony gave him a satisfied smile. She remembered the first email Shawn sent her. Not only was she spending time making a great living, she was about to start living an amazing life.

Then YOU said……….. **So What**

Do you see yourself in Harmony? Describe:

Do you feel that you have to live with a barrier wall up to keep your past from ruining your future? Explain:

Have you wronged others and need to apologize? Will you?

Have you forgiven yourself for your past choices that harmed others?

What are you willing to say **So What** to regarding hurting others?

So What

Ashlyn

So What

Ashlyn

Ashlyn and Melissa had been the best of friends dating back to when they were in elementary school. They grew up on the same street and developed an unbreakable bond ever since the day that Melissa beat up Lil Joey Roberts for trying to steal Ashlyn's brand-new bicycle. Melissa saw Ashlyn as the sister she never had and she made sure no one ever hurt her. While growing up, Ashlyn and Melissa spent quite a bit of time together. They talked for hours, planning their future. Melissa described their lives in great detail. They would attend the same college. They would work in the same company. They would marry best friends and their kids would be best friends. Their lives would be perfect and lived out together. As they grew up, Ashlyn and Melissa remained inseparable. But there was one ominous disparity in their friendship, Ashlyn loved Melissa. Ashlyn was Melissa's biggest cheerleader. Ashlyn looked up to Melissa and counted herself lucky to have her as her closest friend. But Melissa secretly envied everything about Ashlyn. Any time Ashlyn made it in the spotlight, Melissa would find subtle ways to dim her shine. When Ashlyn wanted to try out for the lead in the school play, Melissa criticized her size, voice, and acting skills. Because of Melissa, Ashlyn constantly settled for being a spectator in the audience. When Quentin James asked Ashlyn to the movies, Melissa told Ashlyn a vicious lie about Quentin that made Ashlyn cancel her date. When Melissa received one college acceptance letter to her local university, she successfully talked Ashlyn into turning down the many offers she received from across the country and stayed close to home as well. In Ashlyn's eyes, Melissa always looked out for her, wanting the best for her. In Melissa's eyes, Ashlyn was her best friend who she felt deserved everything that the world had to offer – just as long as it wasn't better than anything Melissa wanted.

So What

After graduating from high school, both ladies attended the same university in their small hometown. They knew most people on campus but stayed near each other. They joined the same organizations and thoroughly enjoyed their college lives. They dated men but no one seriously. They remained focused on their plan for their future.

During their junior year, Ashlyn was swept off her feet by a tall, slender, magnificent looking man named Jason Cooper. He attended the university on an athletic and academic scholarship. To Ashlyn, he was a sexy brainiac. Melissa investigated everything there was to know about Jason. She made sure he was worthy of loving her friend. Melissa approved of Jason and the three became best friends. Ashlyn and Jason's romance intensified. Jason was head over heels in love and he knew he wanted to spend the rest of his life with her. Jason never took her for granted. He always found ways to surprise her. Whether it was having her favorite flowers delivered to her at unexpected times or swooping her up for spontaneous road trips to anywhere, Jason made sure he let Ashlyn constantly know that she meant the world to him. As graduation approached for the three, Melissa was offered a job that she could not pass up. She would be the associate director of a major company on the west coast. She would earn a six-figure salary, enticing benefits and vacation package and an opportunity to advance to higher positions. This was a dream come true for Melissa. She spoke a million miles a minute as she described her new life to Ashlyn. Ashlyn squealed in pure delight, genuinely excited for her friend.

"It's going to be really cool to see all the fantasies we used to talk about finally come true. Working by each other. Living by each other. Our kids raised as best friends. I'm so excited."

Ashlyn gave her a half-smile. "O honey, I haven't had a chance to talk to you with finals, graduation and all. I'm moving to Washington, D.C. with Jason. He was offered a job as communications director for the Crandall Corporation. Once we get settled, we'll get married. He wants me to be a full-time mom to our kids when we start having them. But you know I'll visit often. Can't live life without my girl. Now let's grab something to eat to celebrate. I'm hungry".

Melissa felt as if a speeding eighteen-wheeler ran her over. That was not the plan. That is not what they spent countless hours discussing. That was NOT how THEIR life was supposed to turn out. Melissa kept a pleasant smile on her face, but inside, she was seething. She was angry. She was pissed. How could her best

So What

friend choose a man over her? Melissa had been Ashlyn's protector forever. Anything Ashlyn needed; Melissa made sacrifices to provide. Ashlyn was the only real friend that Melissa had and life apart was not something Melissa would accept.

Soon after graduation, Jason moved to D.C. to find a place to live and get started working. Ashlyn was scheduled to follow soon after once she finished helping Melissa move into her new apartment. Late one evening, Melissa and Ashlyn sat on the patio, sipping a glass of wine and crunching on chips. Ashlyn gave details of her future wedding and hopes for her new life as a wife. Her smile sparkled as she shared step by step what her plans would be once she settled in. Her eyes danced as she gushed over the qualities that Jason had that swept her off her feet. She felt goosebumps on her arms as she said her upcoming married name over and over again, "Mrs. Ashlyn Cooper."

"He's been cheating on you." Melissa harshly told Ashlyn. Melissa's words pierced through Ashlyn's heart like a sword. Burning tears filled her eyes and a golf ball size lump filled her throat. There was no way Jason cheated on her. He loved her way too much. They planned their future together. When Jason's mother died, Ashlyn laid with him for hours, consoling him. When she was nearly kicked out of school because she did not have enough money for tuition, Jason worked extra hours to pay for her semester. They never really argued. They never played mind games. There was never any indication that there were any problems in their relationship.

"Melissa! Why would you say such an awful thing?" Ashlyn gasped between tears.

"I'm sorry to tell you this way. I've known for a long time. I fussed at him once I saw for myself and he swore he would never do it again. I believed him and promised myself I would trust him and let it go. But hearing you talk about him tonight with total joy and love, I just couldn't let you go into this marriage blinded."

Ashlyn sat in silence for what seemed to be an eternity. Melissa refilled her friend's wine glass and told her she was more than welcome to live with her until she decided what to do. She encouraged Ashlyn to block Jason's phone number and not communicate with him. Melissa reminded her that Jason was a sweet-talking charmer and Ashlyn needed time to focus and regroup. Ashlyn agreed.

Over the next few days, Ashlyn went on job interviews and as luck would have it, she was hired at the same company Melissa worked for. Melissa smiled on the outside and turned cartwheels on the inside. Their lives were back on track.

So What

"She's not moving to D.C., Jason," Melissa said to an emotional Jason. After spending countless hours and days calling Ashlyn's phone with no answer, he called Melissa.

"I don't get it. She was only supposed to help you get settled in, then come home to me. What happened that drastically where she found a job and left me? Why won't she talk to me? I just don't understand."

"Look, she never wanted to be a housewife staying at home, cooking, cleaning, raising kids. She never wanted to be the submissive woman supporting her man. She has huge dreams and goals to be a leader. A game-changer. The boss. If you weren't so selfish and self-centered, you would know that. Look, you're a cool guy and I know you'll find someone else who wants that life. Take care and don't call her anymore."

Melissa rudely hung up on Jason, leaving him crushed, bruised, angry, and confused.

Over time, Melissa excelled in her department at work. She received bonuses and promotions that made her stand out amongst her peers. Unbeknownst to Ashlyn, she remained in her entry-level position thanks to the clever manipulation of Melissa. One evening, Melissa was invited to attend a cocktail dinner with some of their company's elite. The owner of the company wanted to spend time with his superstar employees. Melissa invited Ashlyn as her plus one. The ladies knew they had to dress to impress.

"I'm so excited," squealed Melissa as she and Ashlyn danced around their apartment, getting dressed. They had a hard time picking an outfit that would not stand out too much but would not cause them to blend in with everyone else. Ashlyn settled on a hunter green satin halter dress that stopped just above her knee. She wore strappy gold sandals, a gold choker around her neck, dangling gold earrings and her hair pulled back in a sleek ponytail. She looked stunning.

Melissa played it safe with a black cocktail dress that flowed to her calves. An eye-catching split stopped right below her thigh. She wore a beautiful jeweled necklace with matching earrings. She pinned up one side of her cascading curls. Both ladies looked like they were models for a magazine cover. When they stepped into the banquet room where the dinner was held, everyone in the room seemed to stop talking and gaze upon the beauties who walked through the door. Ashlyn and Melissa were uncomfortable at first but then strutted across to the owner confidently to introduce themselves. Grant Mitchell was breathtaking. His

So What

muscular frame towered over the ladies. He firmly shook both women's hands, flashed his pearly white smile, and rubbed his hand through his salt and pepper hair. Although he was professionally attentive to both women, he was obviously attracted to Melissa. When he introduced the ladies to the room's power players, he gently placed his hand on Melissa's lower back and stood close to her. She became intoxicated with the aroma from his cologne. Ashlyn tried not to giggle as she watched her friend squirm to get comfortable next to this stunning man. The mutual attraction was undeniable.

Soft jazz music played in the background and Grant took Melissa by her hand and led her to the dance floor. They stared into each other's eyes and swayed back and forth the rest of the night. Ashlyn smiled as she watched her best friend be fawned over. Melissa never really had any serious romantic relationships. She always found ways to sabotage her own love life. It was as if she was scared or just plain uninterested in committed relationships. Ashlyn nodded her head to the beat of the music and hoped that her friend would let Grant love her.

"He asked me to marry him!" Melissa ran inside Ashlyn's room and jumped in her bed. Ashlyn was completely asleep and woke up groggy, trying to piece together what was going on. Melissa and Grant had been dating for eight months.

Grant surprised Melissa with a romantic getaway to Exuma, Bahamas. They spent time swimming in a lagoon and lounging on the beach. In the middle of a conversation about their next business move, Grant turned towards Melissa and asked if she would be his partner for life. She lifted her sunshades to get a better look at his face. Tears welled up in his eyes as he asked her to marry him. She shot straight up out of her lounge chair, straddled his lap and gently kissed his lips while whispering yes over and over again.

He pushed her back and said, "I'm glad you said yes because I wouldn't have been able to return this." He reached inside his backpack and pulled out a black velvet box. He opened it up and presented her with the biggest diamond ring that she had ever seen.

Ashlyn pounced out of her bed and ran around their apartment, screaming. She was so excited for her friend that she started crying. Melissa walked over to her and bent down on one knee. She took off her ring and placed it on Ashlyn's finger. Ashlyn immediately stopped crying and looked very confused. Melissa said, with a straight face, "Ash, we have been the best of friends all of our lives. And I can't

So What

imagine my life without you. Will you please make me the happiest woman on Earth and be my maid of honor?"

Ashlyn playfully pushed Melissa away and started running around the apartment, waving the ring on her finger and singing, "I'm THE maid of honor."

The ladies spent months planning a wedding that would surpass that of a king and queen. Ashlyn played an intricate role in selecting the wedding dress, the bridesmaids' dresses, the flowers, venue, menu and even helped Melissa write her vows. Ashlyn loved Melissa and was thrilled to see her fairy tale life come together.

Melissa's job assignments allowed her to travel extensively around the world, leaving very little time to spend with Ashlyn. With Melissa's manipulating ways on the other side of the planet, Grant was able to see Ashlyn's talents and gave her more responsibilities and money. Grant assigned Ashlyn to help the company with acquisition projects. Ashlyn was instructed to fly to Washington, D.C. to sign contracts to purchase a fledgling firm that had great potential for growth. Ashlyn walked into the conference room to meet with the board of directors. As she shook each of their hands, she was blown away as she was greeted with a smile by the final director. Jason!

A whirlwind of emotions flooded inside her, but she had to remain professional and composed. After all the contracts were signed, Ashlyn stood up and walked towards the elevators. As the doors were closing, Jason rushed inside. He turned to face her.

"You are so beautiful." He leaned in to kiss her softly on the lips. She did not back away. She missed him tremendously.

"May I take you to dinner?"

She nodded, yes.

They stared at each other across the table. They made small talk about their current lives only. Neither one of them wanted to bring up the past. They talked and laughed until the restaurant closed. Jason drove her to her hotel. They gave each other a tight hug and went their separate ways. With all of the excitement of planning the wedding and coordinating the new business acquisition, Ashlyn did not have time to tell Monica she bumped into Jason. Ashlyn began spending more time in D.C. and with Jason to make sure the business transition went smoothly. The more time Ashlyn and Jason spent together, the more they realized they were falling back in love. As luck would have it, Grant called Ashlyn into his office one day. He was very impressed with how she handled the D.C. office and wanted to

So What

know if she would like to move out there to become its chief executive officer. Without hesitation, she said yes. The only call she made was to Jason. He made arrangements to fly to her and help her move. Melissa had been conducting business out of the country and had no idea of the major changes that were happening to her best friend. Melissa called Ashlyn to make dinner plans for when she returned to the country. Ashlyn was excited and said she had so much to tell her. Melissa arrived at their apartment and walked into packed boxes stacked in the living room. Movers were pushing past her to bring Ashlyn's items to a waiting moving truck downstairs. She looked confused and called Ashlyn's name. Jason walked out of the bedroom to greet her. Melissa stared stunned at him and became instantly furious.

"What is HE doing here?" she growled in between her gritted teeth.

Ashlyn did not notice Melissa's attitude. "I have so much to tell you. I can't wait for dinner. I'm starving. Get the keys, Jason, so we can go."

"He's not coming with us. What are you doing? What are you thinking? WHY IS HE HERE?"

Ashlyn stared at Melissa in shock.

"I told you we had a lot of catching up to do. Grant asked me to oversee the transition of the new offices in D.C. Jason happens to work for the company we acquired. He and I have been working together lately and fell back in love. I am moving to D.C. to be the chief executive officer and to be with Jason. So what's your problem?" Ashlyn stared intensely into Melissa's eyes, not understanding why her friend was not overjoyed for her.

"Ash, this is a big mistake. I'll talk to Grant to keep you here."

"Melissa, I'm moving to D.C. You are getting married and moving on with your life. I am doing the same."

"You can't go. That's not our plan. I don't want to have to say this, but you need to choose between Jason and me."

Ashlyn let out a laugh from deep in her belly. She grabbed her keys, stared at Melissa and said, "Let's go Jason, I'm hungry." Ashlyn slammed the door behind her, leaving Melissa standing near the boxes furious.

At dinner, Ashlyn began to vent. Not understanding why Melissa could not let her move on with Jason.

"Now, if I can forgive you for cheating on me, why can't she?"

Jason lifted his head with a puzzled look. "I NEVER cheated on you."

So What

"But Melissa told me she caught you. That's why I didn't move back to D.C. or return your phone calls."

Jason's face tightened. "She told me that you changed your mind and didn't want to marry me."

They reached across the table and grasped each other's hand, hearts pained by their breakup that was caused by her best friend.

Ashlyn backed out of Melissa's wedding and made plans to move full steam ahead to D.C. Melissa felt as if her world was collapsing. She had to do something drastic to keep her best friend near her. Ashlyn was in her office working to finalize last-minute details of contracts before her move. She received a message from Melissa stating that Jason was cheating again. Melissa wanted Ashlyn to go to their apartment immediately to catch him in the act. Ashlyn got angry at Melissa for sinking so low to keep her and Jason apart. She picked up her phone and called him. His phone kept going straight to voicemail. Ashlyn's heart started pounding. She rushed out of her office and headed straight home. Without making much noise, she opened her apartment door and tiptoed to her bedroom. Sure enough, Jason was sleeping in bed with another woman .... Melissa!

Ashlyn grabbed Melissa by her hair and yanked her out the bed. Ashlyn's fist drew blood as she pounded Melissa's face over and over. Jason woke up startled and tried to pull the women apart. Ashlyn used all the force within her to punch him in his face and knock him into her bedroom wall. She stood over her best friend and stared. She began to feel a pain that she never felt before. Her heart broke into pieces. Not because Jason cheated on her. No, no. She was betrayed by the only person on Earth to whom she gave her complete trust. Melissa was her friend. Her best friend. Her confidant. Her protector. Melissa was her hero who always pushed Ashlyn towards her goals. Tears fell down Ashlyn's face as she clawed at Melissa's face. How would she ever survive the ultimate pain of being stabbed in the back by her best friend?

Jason yelled loudly to get the fighting women's attention. He was confused as to what was going on. Why was Ashlyn attacking Melissa? Why did she punch him? Why was Melissa in bed with him? He demanded to know what was going on. After a long time of deafening silence, Melissa finally conceded and admitted the truth. Jason never cheated on Ashlyn. Not in the past. Not on that night. Melissa was desperate to find a way to keep Ashlyn near her. She initially tried to make Grant change his mind about sending Ashlyn to D.C. He wouldn't budge

So What

on his decision. She tried to talk reason to Ashlyn, but she would not listen. The only other alternative was to hurt Ashlyn's heart again. It worked the last time. Jason was innocently sleeping in Ashlyn's bed with headphones in his ears when Melissa got home. Her conniving mind knew that was the perfect time to stage an affair. All she wanted was for Ashlyn to see for herself that Jason was not good for her. She knew Ashlyn would not be mad at HER. They were best friends. But she would leave Jason for good and would need her best friend to help her through her breakup again.

Ashlyn stared silently in utter disbelief. How could her oldest and dearest friend betray her again? Again? Why didn't Melissa want her to live a happy life? Why was Melissa constantly manipulating Ashlyn? Ashlyn's heart was shattered. Jason walked over to her and gently kissed her forehead. She sobbed in his chest. Melissa continued to try to justify her actions and did not understand why Ashlyn was being so stubborn. Jason took Ashlyn's hand and walked away. Ashlyn slammed their apartment door behind them, knowing she would never see Melissa again.

Ashlyn settled into life in D.C. with Jason. She was still struggling with being betrayed by her best friend. She did not know how to bounce back or how to trust again. This was definitely a test that she was not passing. Her mom visited D.C. to offer support. Ashlyn spent countless hours wallowing in self-pity and complaining that she would be alone for the rest of her life. No best friend. No life.

Jason tried to reason with her. She would not listen. Jason tried to empathize with her, but she would not accept it. Jason tried everything he could to make her snap out of her fog and move on from that hurt. She just kept rejecting him. Her mom got fed up and gave her an old-fashioned tongue lashing.

"Ashlyn Marie. I'm sick and tired of you complaining and griping. There are billions of people on this planet. You were betrayed by one. You cannot give up on friendships based on the stupidity of one. Melissa is a possessive, self-centered idiot. **So what** she destroyed her relationship with you! It's HER loss, NOT yours. You are an amazing woman. Smart, beautiful, ambitious, and loving. Anyone would be blessed to have you in their lives. Melissa knows how valuable you are. Why do you think she became a conniving snake? She always manipulated your friendship to keep you near her. She found a way to sabotage every good thing that was for you that didn't include her. She destroyed her life with that incredible man that was going to marry her just because she couldn't stand to see you happy.

So What

Something is wrong with her, not you. You have so much to offer the world and don't you forget it. You will find new friends. You have a great one here with you now who has been patiently waiting to marry you. A man who only has eyes for you. You will get through this. You will need help, though. Melissa found ways to chip away at your esteem- a little piece at a time. You will need to talk to someone. A counselor or therapist who can help you rebuild you. Someone who can help you cope and move past this betrayal. Someone who can help you heal your wounded heart so you won't be scared to trust again. There is a great doctor in town who could help you. Her name is Dr. Sydney. Call her tomorrow to set up your appointment. Now go clean yourself up and let's grab something to eat. I'm hungry."

Ashlyn glanced back and forth from her mom to Jason. Vivid memories from her childhood through adulthood flashed before her eyes. Yes, her mom was right. Melissa had always found a way to keep Ashlyn near her by sabotaging everything that Ashlyn wanted. Ashlyn realized her self-worth was tied up in her friendship with Melissa and she missed out on opportunity after opportunity because of her blind devotion to Melissa. Yes, her mom was right. Ashlyn was a brilliant and beautiful friend. And Melissa could not deny it. Melissa was lucky to have her as a real friend, but she destroyed it. Ashlyn had to let go of that pain and allow those wounds to heal.

She had other people in her life who valued the treasure that she was... including the man who was standing across the room from her. The man who adored her since the day he met her in college.

Ashlyn walked up to Jason. Planted the softest kiss on his lips. Stared deeply into his eyes and asked, "So when is this wedding?" Jason gave her the biggest smile and said, "We'll talk about that later. Let's go eat. I'm hungry".

Then YOU said.......... **So What**

Do you see yourself in Ashlyn? Describe:

Have you ever been betrayed by a friend? How did you handle it?

So What

What type of qualities do you demand in a valuable friendship?

Are you a good friend? What qualities about you make that true?

What are you willing to say **So What** to regarding friendships?

So What

Tiny

So What

Tiny

"You're really pretty for a big girl."
"Your face is cute but..."
"When is your baby due?"
"You'll never get a man until you lose that weight."

Tabitha "Tiny" Moore heard insensitive comments all of her life. She's always been overweight. She came out of her mother's womb larger than most babies. She was the largest person in her family. She was the largest kid in her school. She was the largest kid on the playground. She was reminded about it constantly through relentless bullying. During recess, she often played alone. Lindsay Gordon warned everyone to stay away from her because she may trip and fall on one of them and kill them. During lunch, she often ate alone. Anthony Turner made loud cow noises every time she took a bite and joked that she needed to join the rest of the herd in the pasture. She never let her classmates see her cry. She would often laugh at the jokes that made fun of her. But on the inside, Tiny was shattered. At such a young age, she did not know why everyone was so mean to her. She was very kind. She was very smart. She was really compassionate. She was a lot of fun. She could be a best friend if someone would give her a chance to be their friend.

"Who needs friends?" her drunk father scoffed one day. "You have family who love ya. You have a mamma who feed ya and a daddy who works hard and makes enough money to be able to feed ya. You got brothers and sisters and cousins and .... You got a lot of people in your family who love you no matter how fat you are. One day we know you're gonna lose that weight. That's why we call ya Tiny. Using that law of attraction to speak it to the universe." Tiny managed to give a fake smile and hugged her daddy's neck.

Her Uncle Andrew let out a hearty laugh. "Your dad is drunk, Tiny, but he means well. You are stunning, no matter what size you are. You're going to have

So What

to be mentally stronger than most kids. People are cruel and insensitive. They don't realize or care how much their words hurt. You have to understand that you are amazing, Tiny, and you will meet friends who love you for you. And when you get older and have to hire the people who treated you like crap, say there's no room in the pasture for people like you. Then moo. That's how karma works. They'll need you before you'll need them. Now, if you love me, squeeze my neck and bring some beers to the garage for me and your daddy."

Uncle Andrew wasn't really Tiny's uncle. He had been their neighbor for years. He didn't have a family of his own, so he made himself an honorary member of Tiny's family. He was Tiny's biggest cheerleader. Always complimenting her and encouraging her.

Tiny was an exceptional student. She studied hard and was always on the honor roll. Tiny was also an exceptional athlete. Despite her size, she excelled in swimming and wrestling. She often won first place awards in science fairs, debate contests, and oratory contests. Every time she stepped on stage to accept her awards, her family would cheer. Her classmates would moo. During her school's regional swim match, she placed second. When she stepped on the winner's platform to receive her medal, the audience cheered, her classmates mooed. Throughout the years of ridicule, Tiny kept a smile on her face. Throughout her years of ridicule, Uncle Andrew was there to encourage her to keep moving forward and not let the stupidity of others hurt her feelings. Uncle Andrew never knew that he prevented Tiny from taking her own life many times. He always seemed to show up at just the right time and said just the right words to help her make it through. Uncle Andrew was her living angel.

When Tiny was a sophomore in high school, she began to make friends. She was invited to parties and group dates. It seemed that they could finally see past her weight and get to know the incredible person she was. She finally began to enjoy her social life. Ursula Flemming, who was THE elite girl in their school, was planning for her fabulously over the top pool party. Tiny was stunned and excited to receive an invitation in the mail. She asked her mom to take her shopping for a swimsuit. Her mom said, "Definitely not. It's fine that you wear swimsuits when you're competing, but when you're just hanging out with regular-sized people, you need to wear clothes. You don't want all those pretty girls making fun of you." Although the way she said it was hurtful, Tiny knew her mom meant well.

So What

Tiny mentioned the conversation to Uncle Andrew. He shook his head and laughed at Tiny's mom. "Lord knows your family loves you to death. They just weren't blessed with a conversation filter. You can wear whatever you like. You just have to know how to select the right fit for your size. I'll pick you up from school tomorrow to take you shopping."

After school, Uncle Andrew drove Tiny to a nice clothing store which specialized in plus size clothes. Tiny modeled several styles of bathing suits that looked amazing on her. Uncle Andrew selected two and treated her to a pair of lovely sandals. Tiny hugged Uncle Andrew's neck and thanked him for loving her the way he did. Uncle Andrew kissed her on her cheek and said he never had children, but he would have a football team full of kids just like Tiny if he did. She blushed.

The day of the party was exciting for Tiny. She did not dare let her mom know she was wearing her swimsuit underneath the long dress her mom forced her to wear. She pulled her hair back in a ponytail, put on a huge floppy hat, sunshades, and the cute sandals that Uncle Andrew bought her. She walked into the living room to wait on her dad to drive her to the party. Her mom looked her up and down, then smiled approvingly. Tiny loved her family.

Tiny arrived at the party and kissed her dad on his cheek. He told her to have a great time and he would pick her up at midnight. Tiny was greeted by her friends with hugs and giggles. Lola looked at Tiny in that long, unflattering dress and said, "Girl, I know you not wearing THAT ugly dress to THIS fabulous party."

Tiny laughed, "No. You know my mom is extra mom-ish. I got my bathing suit on under this." Her friends led her to the pool house to get pool party ready. They squealed and smiled as Tiny revealed the beautiful swimsuit that Uncle Andrew picked out. They told her she looked great, grabbed her by her hand and led her to the party. No one seemed to care about Tiny's size in a swimsuit. Everyone was genuinely having a great time. Tiny took a few laps in the pool as her friends tossed beach balls and splashed each other with water. This was the most fun that Tiny had ever had in her life.

As the evening moved on, some of the boys brought out alcohol for everyone to enjoy. Anthony Turner and two of his friends drank more than anyone else at the party, and they began groping the girls and acting obnoxious. He saw Tiny and started mooing. His drunk friends joined in. Lola's boyfriend walked up to Anthony and told him to control himself or be escorted off the property. Anthony

So What

and his drunk friends stumbled into a corner and mooed in a whisper and laughed. Tiny enjoyed her time with her friends. They laughed and danced and ate lots of food. Despite being harassed by stupid Anthony and his drunk friends, Tiny was having a great time.

Tiny went inside the house to grab her phone. She begged her parents to let her stay just a little while longer since she was having so much fun. Her parents agreed to an extra hour. Tiny headed back outside but was startled to see Anthony and his friends standing near her. Anthony asked to talk to her to apologize for his behavior. He took her by her hand and walked to a quiet section of the house. He told her he was a jerk and wanted her forgiveness. He walked slowly to her. She began to feel uncomfortable, so she quickly said she forgave him and tried to walk back to the party. Anthony grabbed her arm. She felt a tug on her other arm. Someone had switched off the lights, and Tiny felt a multitude of hands groping her. Anthony and his friends overpowered her. She started screaming, but she could not be heard over the loud music. She started crying, but her tears remained unnoticed. Anthony and his friends took turns brutalizing her. Touching her. Spitting on her. Taunting her. Laughing at her. After what seemed to be an eternity, Anthony and his friends stumbled back to the party and left Tiny sprawled out on the floor, devastatingly bruised inside and out. Tiny sobbed, then began to cry hysterically. She realized no one had bothered to even look for her.

She gathered herself together and went to get her phone. She could not call her parents. She would get fussed at for wearing that bathing suit. She called her Uncle Andrew. Anger rose in him as he listened to Tiny tell her horrendous story in between her tears. He told her to grab her things and wait for him in front of the house. Tiny had to walk through a sea of drunk students to get to the pool house where her clothes were. Anthony and his friends were dunking each other in the pool. When they saw Tiny, they began to moo. Everyone began to laugh. This time, Tiny did not join in. She sat on the curb, waiting for Uncle Andrew. She did not understand why he was so late. She decided to start walking home and she would run into him on the way. Tiny used that alone time to replay that horrible scene over and over again in her head. What did she do wrong? She should not have worn that bathing suit. She began to feel lower than she ever felt in her life. She knew Uncle Andrew would have the right words to say to help her through this madness. She could not wait to hug his neck. He was her angel.

So What

Flashing lights and sirens interrupted her focus. She walked up on a three-car pileup in the road. One car was in flames. The other two were crushed beyond recognition. Emergency personnel rushed to rescue drivers and passengers. Stretchers whisked past Tiny. Body bags were zipped up. Tiny walked a little closer to see the final body bag being zipped over a familiar face. Uncle Andrew.

Tiny felt a sharp pain then coldness. She fainted and collapsed on the cement, hitting her head. Emergency workers rushed her to the hospital, along with the other victims. Tiny could barely understand the whispers of voices surrounding her. She tried to open her eyes but was blinded by lights shining directly on her. She felt pain in her head and soreness throughout her body. She tried to sort through the confusion of what was going on and where she was. Tiny blinked several times to gain her focus. She saw her mom and dad in a corner whispering to a doctor. Her dad's arm was wrapped around her mom's shaking and inconsolable body. The doctor noticed Tiny stirring in her hospital bed and went over to check her vital signs. Tiny stared at her mom, trying to get an understanding of what was going on.

Tiny's heart raced as her dad gave details of that dreadful night. Uncle Andrew was driving somewhere at a high rate of speed. He was not paying attention to his surroundings and plowed into the back of a car that was stopped at a red light. The unsuspecting car was thrown into the path of oncoming traffic. The powerful impact caused the car to burst into flames. Four members of that family burned up in the fire; however, only a son survived. The family in the truck from the oncoming traffic were seriously injured and being cared for several doors down from Tiny. Uncle Andrew died upon impact. Tiny's mom and dad said the investigators were trying to piece together the scene to figure out why Uncle Andrew was driving erratically. Tiny knew why. Her heart began to break into a million pieces. She was the reason Uncle Andrew was speeding. She was the reason he was distracted. She was the reason that the family died. She was the cause of this unspeakable disaster. Now all she wanted to do was fade away and die.

During Uncle Andrew's funeral, Tiny sat emotionless. She felt the stares from everyone who was grieving. Word spread fast that Uncle Andrew was speeding to get Tiny from a party. Rumors spread that Tiny was drunk at the party and got thrown out. That Tiny was being a tramp at the party and got thrown out. That Tiny was fighting at the party and got thrown out. No one ever told the truth…

So What

that Tiny was brutally raped at the party and Uncle Andrew was rushing to rescue her.

Tiny could not believe Uncle Andrew was gone. She could not forgive the fact that she was the cause. She sunk into a dark dismissal place in her mind. She felt worthless. She felt guilty. She felt so much pain. She began to sink into a severe depression and no one could make her snap out of it. No one made an effort to help her through it. Quite the opposite, her family and friends added to her pain. She was frequently blamed for the accident. Her family glared at her with silent judgement. Her classmates taunted her daily with rumors and innuendos of why Tiny called Uncle Andrew to pick her up and not her father. They implied that Uncle Andrew must have really been her boyfriend and found out she was being a slut at the party and was headed to straighten her out. Every scenario told was worse than the previous.

Tiny suffered her way through the remainder of her high school years. She buried herself in her books and earned her spot as the valedictorian of her class. As valedictorian, she was required to prepare the class speech. Tiny dreaded having to stand before her classmates and community. As her name was called, she slowly made her way towards the podium. Her classmates mooed and the audience laughed. Tiny wanted to run out of the auditorium and never be seen again. But she knew Uncle Andrew would be disappointed in her if she let them see her rattled. She lifted her head, quickened her steps, and made her way to the microphone. She began to speak in an eloquent voice. Her words were inspiring and profound. She delivered her speech with confidence. When she finished, she smiled at the audience. Anthony Turner stood up, started to clap, then mooed. His friends stood up and joined him. The audience erupted in laughter. Tiny was humiliated. She hung her head low and returned to her seat. Tiny was awarded several full scholarships to colleges near and far. She chose the college that was the furthest away from the hell she called home.

Although she excelled in college and had a prestigious career as an advisor at an investment firm, she had a hard time coping with life. When she was alone, scenes from her childhood nightmare haunted her mercilessly. She took sleeping pills to try to help her rest. When that did not work, she turned to alcohol and overeating to numb her pain. Over time, that stopped helping. Tiny had no one to confide in who could help her through this torment. Tiny soon found solace in her wealthy clients. She did not care who they were or what their marital status

So What

was. She began to develop an unsavory appetite for no strings attached sex. She felt powerful and in control. Tiny's promiscuity got out of control, to where she did not care that most encounters were one time. She did not care that her romantic escapades went no further than a dark and dank hotel room. She did not care who she seduced. She enjoyed the thrill of the forbidden and craved more.

Tiny was assigned to land the account of one of the wealthiest families in the region. The Davenport's earned their riches through real estate developments. Their former financial advisor was caught stealing from their accounts. They were in a hurry to find someone reputable and trustworthy to handle their fortune. Tiny came highly recommended. Tiny and a senior advisor met with Mr. and Mrs. Davenport. Mrs. Davenport frowned at Tiny. Her piercing green eyes scanned from the top of Tiny's head to the soles of Tiny's shoes as if she was trying to determine if Tiny would rob them blind based on her physical appearance. Mrs. Davenport smiled sinisterly when her gaze fell on Tiny's waist and stomach.

Mrs. Davenport knew she did not have to worry about her husband having wandering eyes or hands if Tiny was hired. "We'll take her." Mrs. Davenport said relatively nonchalantly. Tiny was excited about this opportunity. The money she would make off of this account would help her reach her financial goals much faster. Tiny flashed a bright smile and shook Mr. Davenport's hand, then Mrs. Davenport's hand. Mrs. Davenport pulled Tiny close for a tight hug and whispered, "If you screw over my family or me, I will have you killed." Tiny tried not to show fear on her face, but she was afraid of Mrs. Davenport. For months, Tiny worked hard to analyze the best stocks to invest the Davenport's money. For months, Tiny's actions generated significant returns. The Davenport's recommended more of their wealthy friends to Tiny. She was a strategic genius. She generated vast amounts of money for her clients, her firm, and herself. Although her personal life was in shambles, she made up for it by the best form of therapy … retail therapy. She spent money faster than she could earn it. She did not care. There was more of it to be made.

When it finally seemed as if her life was getting better, Tiny received unexpected news that shattered her world again. Her mother died from a massive heart attack. Tiny had not been home since she moved away after graduation. Although she loved her family, she did not speak to them anymore because she could not stand being judged. She dreaded going home. Flashes of memories began haunting her again. In the days leading up to her trip home, Tiny was grumpy, irritable, and

So What

distracted. She was summoned to the senior advisor's office to discuss her recent behavior. For the first time, Tiny told someone of her heinous childhood and the rape. Tears that had been bottled up for years began to stream down her face. It was obvious that her past weighed her down. The senior advisor demanded that Tiny seek counseling as soon as she got back from her mother's funeral to finally release the pressure she was under and move forward with a peaceful life. Tiny packed for a weeklong stay. When she arrived at the airport, she expected to see a familiar face waiting for her. She saw none even though her family knew what time she was scheduled to arrive. She took a cab to her childhood home. She sat in the back seat, numb. Had she made a mistake by going home? She had not seen any of her family in years. Did it matter if she were there or not? The last funeral she attended was Uncle Andrew's and she certainly did not receive any condolences that day.

When Tiny arrived home, she saw scores of cars and trucks lined along the street. Tiny's heart began to pound in anticipation of how she would be received. She entered the front door without knocking. She stood still surveying the room. So many neighbors who she had not seen in years, wrapped their arms around each other to console one another.

"TINY!" Her dad spotted her and rushed to hug her. He held on for what seemed to be eternity. He began to sob in her arms and repeatedly told her he missed and loved her. She wrapped her arms tight around his neck and whispered that she loved him. During her mother's funeral, Tiny tried to focus on the preacher's sermon, but she was distracted by the familiar faces of those who made her life a living hell. She nearly froze when she caught a glimpse of Anthony Turner, who was seated with his wife and two daughters. Flashbacks from that night caused her skin to crawl and her stomach turned into knots. Her senior advisor was right. She needed therapy to help her get over her past.

Tiny became angry that Anthony moved on with his life while hers was shattered into pieces. How could he sit in the same room as her knowing what he did? At the gravesite, people lined up to hug Tiny and offered their condolences. She plastered a fake smile on her face but inside, she was enraged. These people destroyed her life, but she seemed to be the only one who remembered. She grew angrier inside as the scab that grew over her heart peeled away and exposed a fresh wound. When Tiny returned to work, she could not shake the hatred that she had for everyone who hugged her. Didn't they know what happened to her? Didn't

So What

they care that she lived her whole life in pain? Why was she the only one suffering? Tiny could not tolerate the constant thoughts running through her mind. She could not sleep. She could not focus. She could not function. She turned to the only things that helped her escape her reality - alcohol, food, and sex.

    Tiny's issues began to affect her work performance. Her golden touch began to fade and her poor investment choices cost her clients money, lots of money. Mr. Davenport demanded a meeting with Tiny. He was furious as he reviewed his account with her. He was baffled at Tiny's lack of concern. Little did he know, she was drunk and was trying to look sober. He informed Tiny that he was displeased with her services and would request his account and those of his friends be moved to another advisor. Tiny knew she could not afford to lose clients. She begged and pleaded for Mr. Davenport to give her another chance. He said in his line of work, he could not afford to give second chances. He stood up and walked towards the door. She stood up and rushed over to him. She figured her normal seduction tactics would change his mind. She grabbed his arm and pulled him towards her. She grabbed the back of his neck and pulled his head towards her. She leaned forward to plant her lips on his. She was shocked into reality when Mr. Davenport pushed her away, glared at her with an icy stare, and stormed out the door. Tiny sunk in her office chair and cried for hours.

    The next morning, Tiny received an email from the owner of the company to meet with him that afternoon. Tiny was horrified when she walked into his office and saw Mrs. Davenport. Mrs. Davenport stormed towards Tiny and slapped her face so hard that she left a handprint. Tears streamed down Tiny's face from the pain of the slap and embarrassment of what she did to Mr. Davenport. Tiny zoned out as she watched the owner of the company yell at her about her inappropriate behavior. He said Mrs. Davenport threatened to pull her business and those she referred to the firm unless Tiny was fired immediately. He told Tiny to clear out her office and she would be escorted to her car by security.

    Tiny drove straight to the liquor store to stock up on enough alcohol to make her pass out for days. As she waited in line, she noticed a flyer that advertised free counseling sessions at the local community center for anyone having a hard time with life. Tiny placed the bottles of alcohol on the counter, grabbed the flyer and rushed out the door. She called the number and made plans to attend the group session later that night. When she arrived, she was greeted by a room full of people who were paralyzed by issues of their past just as she was. The group provided a

So What

safe environment for her to open up and give names to the demons that haunted her for years. Rape. Bullying. Alcoholism. Overeating. Promiscuity. Depression. Self-hate. Guilt. Tiny recounted the story of the worst day of her life. She blamed her weight, wearing that bathing suit, and not being strong enough to fight Anthony and his friends off of her that night of her Uncle Andrew's death and the death of the four people in the other car.

She admitted to abusing alcohol, food and sex to help deal with the pain. She admitted to feeling worthless and suicidal because of how others treated her. She admitted to hating Anthony and everyone in her hometown for making her life hell and moving on with their lives without so much as an apology. Tears and sobs consumed Tiny. She felt embarrassed, but she could not stop crying. An arm wrapped around her shoulder. A gentle male voice asked for her real name. She sobbed harder as she stuttered, "Tabitha".

"Hi, Tabitha. My name is Allen. We're glad you're here today and willing to open up to us. We're here to help you move on from your past. You certainly had a hard life, but that shouldn't stop you from looking forward to an amazing future. You're extremely beautiful, Tabitha. Your career path shows that you're extremely intelligent. Yes, those who hurt you moved on and you must move on too. You've spent too many years harboring hatred in your heart for people who may not even remember what they did to you. You've been self-destructive and living in your past. I know it hurts, but you must move forward. Yes, you were teased because of your weight. Yes, you were brutally violated by animals who should've been locked up in jail. Yes, you began to abuse your body with alcohol and risky sex. But **so what**! You're still here. You survived it all. You're strong enough to know you need help and showed up here. You are an amazing woman, Tabitha, and it's time for you to see it for yourself. If you let us, this group will help you."

Tiny had a bittersweet calm overcome her. Those words were words that Uncle Andrew would have said to her. She smiled, thankful that he was still her protective angel. She looked up to smile at Allen and was startled. He was badly disfigured. More than eighty percent of his body was scarred from burns. He had a patch over one eye and wore a prosthetic arm. She asked why he was in the group session and what happened to him. He smiled as he recounted the worst night of his life.

"I used to come here to get help with forgiveness. This group literally saved my life. Now I volunteer to help others who are having a hard time with life and use their past hurts as a testimony to help other hurt people heal. On the day before

So What

my sixteenth birthday, my dad decided to surprise me with a trip with my mom and two sisters to a concert featuring my favorite group. He decided to drive straight through without stopping for a hotel so that we could make it to the city and have plenty of time to sightsee. We drove through this small town a little after midnight. We stopped at a red light. The next thing I remember, I was rolling on the street to put out the fire that engulfed me. I heard piercing screams from my family, who were trapped in our car. I couldn't save them. I tried. I couldn't. My family died right in front of me. I struggled for years to forgive myself for not saving my family. I struggled for years to forgive the people who tormented me for the way I looked with burns and scars. I struggled for years to forgive the doctors who couldn't repair my face or save my arm or eye. I struggled for years to forgive the man who caused the wreck that destroyed my life. That was the most challenging part of my forgiveness journey. I forgave him when I found out his story. He was speeding as he rushed to help his niece, who was brutally raped at a party. He was on the phone with the police trying to get them to meet him at the house party to save her. He told the officer his niece's name was Tabitha and his name was Andrew. A few seconds later, he crashed into us.

I found out there were never any charges filed against the rapists because no one would come forward to tell the truth. Not even Tabitha. I began to imagine how difficult it must have been for her to experience every pain of that night. I often thought about the choices my own father would have made were he in Andrew's shoes. I had to seek help to come to grips with everything that happened that night and many nights afterward. I knew I could not live the rest of my life allowing that night to replay like a bad movie over and over again. I had to make a decision. I decided to forgive Andrew and myself. Tabitha, I want to be the one to help you forgive those monsters who you think destroyed your life AND yourself. Will you let me?"

She was beyond shocked that she was face to face with a person whose life was forever changed by what happened to her on that nightmare of a night. She stared past his disfigurement and scars. He was truly at peace. She wanted the same peace. She had to forgive herself. She had to accept his help. She had to make a decision that would ultimately save her life. She gave him a genuine smile and said yes. Despite the horrors of her past, Tiny was able to turn her life around. She found a job paying more than she made at the firm. She began to budget her finances and pay off her debt. She started exercising to become heart healthy. She began to

So What

volunteer at the community center. She found her strength through her past and she used her testimony to help others navigate through their pain. Although she never forgot what was done to her, she forgave everyone involved. Not for them, but for herself. That is what Uncle Andrew would have told her to do. He would be so proud of her right now. She was thankful that her angel was still around to guide her.

Then YOU said……….. **So What**

Do you see yourself in Tiny? Describe:

What trauma have you faced that is holding you hostage today?

How do you compare your life where you were then versus where you are now mentally?

So What

What would it take to get over traumatic experiences that you faced?

If you face trauma in the future, how will you handle it better than you did before?

What are you willing to say **So What** to regarding childhood trauma?

Moving Forward

Anyone who has lived lives similar to **S**ydney, **O**livia Rose, **W**averly, **H**armony, **A**shlyn, or **T**iny understands how difficult it could be to move forward. It would be easy to wrap yourself in a blanket and sleep your days away. It would be easy to drown your sorrows in alcohol, numb your pain with drugs, or stuff your hurt with food. It would be easy to escape your reality with meaningless sexual encounters or simply end your life.

But you were not created to live a mediocre life. You were created to live life more abundantly. You were created to make an impact in this world. You were created to use your testimony to help others like yourself. You were created to be an unstoppable powerhouse.

DO NOT FORGET YOUR PAST. It is a part of your story, an incredible story that will serve as a guide to help others who struggle through the same tragedies that you overcame.

DO NOT FORGET YOUR PAST. It is a part of your journey, an incredible journey that will test your courage to move forward in a world that pushes you around, causing painful bumps and bruises.

DO NOT FORGET YOUR PAST, but do not let it keep you so broken that you are too afraid to venture out and enjoy this amazing life that is designed just for you.

Starting now, you will no longer allow yourself to move forward by walking backwards. It is easy to give up, but you are no quitter. It is easy to hide in order to protect yourself from more hurt, but you are no coward. It is scary to move out of your comfort zone, but releasing the emotional shackles will give you a freedom to enjoy your present and future.

Yes, you have a past

So What

Yes, you were abused
Yes, you were teased
Yes, you were betrayed
Yes, you were left

But **SO WHAT**? You are still here. You still wake up every morning with a new chance to leave your mark in this world. Stop moving forward by walking backwards!
You are strong
You are amazing
You are courageous
You are magnificent
You are gifted
You are loved
You are talented
You are brilliant
You are spectacular
You are a force to be reckoned with
And if anyone is bold enough to say anything differently, shout **SO WHAT** and keep moving forward.

www.ingramcontent.com/pod-product-compliance
Lightning Source LLC
Chambersburg PA
CBHW060212050426
42446CB00013B/3059